D1334556

# Art Directors' Index

## TO ILLUSTRATORS 11

# Credits / Copyright

**Dust jacket illustration**
**Illustration de la jaquette**
**Schutzumschlagillustration**

Thierry Clauson

**Divider page design**
**Design des pages de titre**
**Design der Länder-Seiten**

Priscilla Teoh, FIE-JJA, Singapore

**Production manager**
**Chef de production**
**Produktionsleiter**

Bernard Vouillamoz, Geneva

**Publisher**
**Editeur**
**Verlag**

ROTOVISION SA
Route Suisse 9
CH–1295 Mies
Switzerland
Tel. (0)22-755 30 55
Tlx: 419 246 rovi ch
Fax: (0)22-755 40 72

**Copyright**


ISBN 2-88046-126-X
Printed in Hong Kong

The work of this index is the choice of the Artists and/or their representatives, not of the Publisher.

As this book is printed in four-colour process, a few of the illustrations reproduced here may appear to be slightly different than in their original reproduction.



Le choix des matières dans cet index est le fait des artistes et/ou de leurs représentants et non de l'éditeur.

Ce livre étant imprimé en quadrichromie, de légères différences avec la reproduction originale peuvent apparaître dans certains cas.



Die Arbeit in diesem Buch ist die Wahl der Fotografen/Illustratoren und/oder ihrer Agenten, und nicht des Verlages.

Da dieses Buch im Vierfarbendruck hergestellt ist, können gegenüber der Original-Reproduktion kleinere Differenzen vorkommen.

# Content / Contenu / Inhalt

## NORTH AMERICA



## LATIN AMERICA



## AUSTRALASIA



## ASIA



## SOUTH-EAST ASIA



## EUROPE



### BENELUX



### SCANDINAVIA

# Portfolio Page Sales Agents

**AMERICA**
AMERICAN SHOWCASE INC.
724 Fifth Avenue
New York, NY 10019
Tel. 212-245 0981
Fax: 212-265 2247
Contact: Marie-Christine Matter

**ARGENTINA**
DOCUMENTA SRL.
Aquiles Ferrario
Cordoba 612 entrepiso
1054 Buenos Aires
Tel. 1-322 9581
Fax: 1-111 879
Tlx: 24051 schnk ar

**AUSTRALIA**
ARMADILLO PUBLISHERS PTY LTD
205/207 Scotchmer Street
Fitzroy North
Victoria 3068
Tel. 03-489 95 59
Fax: 03-489 5576
Tlx: 30834 displa aa

**AUSTRIA**
Gudrun Tempelmann-Boehr
Am Rosenbaum 7
4006 Erkrath
Deutschland
Tel. 0211-25 32 46
39 68 39
Fax: 0211-25 46 32

**BELGIUM**
SEDIP
Mr. P. de Vanssay / Mrs E. Wibaut
Rue Vanderkindere 318
1180 Bruxelles
Tel. 2-343 44 99
Fax: 2-343 79 51

**BRAZIL**
CASA ONO COMÉRCIO
E IMPORTAÇÃO LTDA.
Rua Fernão Dias 492 – Pinheiros
São Paulo
CEP 05427
Tel. 11-813 6522
Fax: 11-813 6921
Tlx: 11-80901 ono br

**CANADA**
CREATIVE SOURCE
WILCORD PUBLICATIONS LTD
511 King St. W, Suite 110
Toronto, Ontario
M5V 2Z4
Tel. (416) 599-5797
Fax: (416) 591-1630
Contact: Geoff Cannon

**CHILI**
BLACKBOX
M.H. Theurillat
Perez Valenzuela 1503
Santiago
Tel. 2-223 2869
Fax: 2-274 7520
Tlx: 645 330 booth

**COLOMBIA**
FONDO CULTURAL IBEROAMERICANO
H. Tinjaca
Calle 66 A N.° 16-41
Apartado 51340
Bogotá D.E.
Tel. 249 77 69
Fax: 283 02 65
611 08 07

**DENMARK**
DANSK CELEBRATION
Danish Forlags Service
Orbækvej 739
52220 Odense SO
Tel. 65 97 24 06
Fax: 66 17 74 42
Contact: Helen Ramsdal

**FINLAND**
Leena Anttila
Kilonkallio 7 A
P.O. Box 50
02610 Espoo
Tel. 509 30 11
Fax: 59 20 49

**FRANCE**
ROTOVISION SA
Route Suisse 9
CH–1295 Mies
Switzerland
Tel. (0)22-755 30 55
Fax: (0)22-755 40 72
Tlx: 419 246 rovi ch

**GERMANY**
Gudrun Tempelmann-Boehr
Am Rosenbaum 7
4006 Erkrath
Tel. 0211-25 32 46
39 68 39
Fax: 0211-25 46 32

Manfred Ostner
Kaiserplatz 3
8000 München 40
Tel. 089-39 88 58

**HOLLAND**
SEDIP
Mr. P. de Vanssay / Mrs E. Wibaut
Rue Vanderkindere 318
1180 Bruxelles
Belgium
Tel. 2-343 44 99
Fax: 2-343 79 51

**HONG KONG**
KENG SENG TRADING & CO.
David Chen
Loong San Building – Room 103
140-142 Connaught Road
Central
Hong Kong
Tel. 5-45 50 08
Fax: 5-41 40 25
Tlx: 64820 kshk hx

**INDIA**
GS BOOKS INTERNATIONAL
Mr. K.S. Ganesh
503 Amit Industrial Estate
61 Dr. S.S. Rao Road, Lalbaug
Bombay 400 012
Tel. 413 81 42
Tlx: 117 2336 baas in

**INDONESIA**
PT GRAFINDO INTER PRIMA
32 Kwitang Road
P.O. Box 4215
Jakarta
Tel. 21- 36 39 21
Fax: 21-858 18 06
Tlx: 45366 gps ia

**ITALY**
ROTOVISION SA
Route Suisse 9
CH–1295 Mies
Switzerland
Tel. (0)22-755 30 55
Fax: (0)22-755 40 72
Tlx: 419 246 rovi ch

**JAPAN**
ORION BOOKS
ORION SERVICE & TRADING
CO. LTD.
Hideo Kaneko
Papyrus Building
58 Kanda-Jimbocho 1-chome
Chiyoda-ku
Tokyo 101
Tel. 295 4008
Fax: 295 4366
Tlx: 24408 orionagy j

**KOREA**
DESIGN HOUSE
186-210 Jang-Choong-Dong
2-Ga, Choong-ku
100-392 Seoul
Tel. 275 6151
Fax: 275 7884

**LUXEMBOURG**
SEDIP
Mr. P. de Vanssay / Mrs E. Wibaut
Rue Vanderkindere 318
1180 Bruxelles
Belgium
Tel. 2-343 44 99
Fax: 2-343 79 51

**MALAYSIA**
FLO ENTERPRISE SDN. BHD.
Ong Kah Khin
42-A Jalan SS21/58
Damansara Utama
Selangor
Tel. 03-718 7770
718 7790
Fax: 03-718 6426

**MEXICO**
PRODUCCIÓN MGA S.A.
Marcela Gaxiola
Montes Cárpatos 210
Col. Lomas Virreyes
11000 México, D.F.
Tel. 540 20 76
Fax: 525 01 91

**NEW ZEALAND**
PROPAGANDA
123 Ponsonby Road
Ponsonby
Auckland
Tel. 09-781 582
Fax: 09-781 582
Contact: Stuart Shepherd

**NORWAY**
TW MARKETING
Thor Willy Bjerke
Fougstadsgate 22 B
0173 Oslo 1
Tel. 02-37 50 80
Fax: 02-37 73 20

**PORTUGAL**
LIBROS TÉCNICOS LDA.
Pedro Campos
Rua Herois Dadra 2-1.º DT
Damaia
2700 Amadora – Lisboa
Tel. 011-97 05 59
97 24 39
Fax: 011-67 84 89

**SINGAPORE**
PAGE ONE – THE DESIGNER'S
BOOKSHOP PTE LTD
Mark Tan
6 Raffles Boulevard
03-128 Marina Square
Singapore 1030
Tel. 339 0288
Fax: 339 9828

**SPAIN**
ROVIRA ASOCIADOS SL
Calle Galileo 288 Entresuelo B
08024 Barcelona
Tel. 93-490 57 34
Fax: 93-490 16 62

**SWEDEN**
ROTOVISION SA
Route Suisse 9
CH–1295 Mies
Switzerland
Tel. (0)22-755 30 55
Fax: (0)22-755 40 72
Tlx: 419 246 rovi ch

**SWITZERLAND**
ROTOVISION SA
Route Suisse 9
CH–1295 Mies
Tel. (0)22-755 30 55
Fax: (0)22-755 40 72
Tlx: 419 246 rovi ch

**THAILAND**
AB PUBLICATIONS
Ramesh Shrestha
131/26-28 Sukhumvit 9
Bangkok 10110
Tel. 253 2561
Fax: 253 2561

**UNITED KINGDOM**
ROTOVISION SA
c/o HOT SALES INTERNATIONAL LTD
35 Britannia Row
London N1 8QH
Tel. 071-226 1739
Fax: 071-226 1540

**VENEZUELA**
CONTEMPORÁNEA DE EDICIONES SRL
Luis Fernando Ramirez
Av. La Salle cruce con Lima
Edificio Irbia
Urb. Los Caobos
Apartado Aéreo
1020 Caracas
Tel. 2-782 2991
2-782 3320
Fax: 2-782 3431
Tlx: 29105 armun

# Index

## Australia
## Australie
## Australien



## Austria
## Autriche
## Österreich



## Belgium
## Belgique
## Belgien

## Canada
## Canada
## Kanada

**BEHA, PHILIPPE 74**
5193 rue Cartier
Montréal, Québec
H2H 1X6
Tél. (514) 843-3218
Fax: (514) 843-3219

**BERKSON, NINA 75**
400 Dowd
Montréal, Québec
Tél. (514) 878-2359

**CLAF / CLAUDE LAFRANCE 76**
5340 Louis-Joseph Doucet
Montréal, Québec
H1M 3J9
Tél. (514) 255-3929

**ELSOM, VICKY 77**
95 Lawton Blvd.
Toronto, Ontario
M4V 1Z8
Tel. (416) 489-6453

**JOHANNSEN, ROBERT 86**
7251 Copenhagen Road #62
Mississauga, Ontario
L5N 2H6
Tel. (416) 567-1493

**MACDOUGALL, ROB 78**
2049 Lakeshore Road West
Oakville, Ontario
L6L 1G6
Tel. (416) 847-7663

**MASSICOTTE, ALAIN 79**
1121 rue Ste-Catherine Ouest #400
Montréal, Québec
H3B 1J5
Tél. (514) 843-4169
Fax: (514) 849-5955

**MORIN, PAUL 80**
RR #4
Rockwood, Ontario
N0B 2K0
Tel. (416) 833-9906

**NORMANDIN, LUC 82**
5031 rue Sherbrooke Ouest
Suite 9
Montréal, Québec
H4A 1S8
Tél. (514) 489-1172

**ONE A.M. 84**
33 Wasdale Crescent #9
Toronto, Ontario
M6N 1N9
Tel. (416) 782-5113

**ROBERTS, BRUCE 81, 83**
60 de Brésoles #205
Montréal, Québec
H2Y 1V5
Tél. (514) 849-1001

**STUCK, MARION 85**
7251 Copenhagen Road #62
Mississauga, Ontario
Tel. (416) 567-1493

**TATE, JOHN 87**
164 Poplar Drive
Dollard des Ormeaux, Québec
H9A 2A7
Tel. (514) 684-1906

**WEBER, GORDON 88**
6 Nanook Crescent
Kanata, Ontario
K2L 2A7
Tel. (613) 592-8826

## Chile
## Chili
## Chile

**FUENTES, LINCOLN 91**
Hamburgo 365-Y
Nuñoa
Santiago
Tel. 227 11 90

## Germany
## Allemagne
## Deutschland

**BORDICH, GEERT 192**
Eschenweg 3
2082 Tornesch
Tel. 04122-5 21 51

Agent:
GUDRUN TEMPELMANN-BOEHR
Am Rosenbaum 7
4006 Erkrath
Tel. 0211-25 46 32

**GERHARDT, FRANK 196**
Johannisstrasse 36
4800 Bielefeld 1
Tel. 0521-87 43 88
Fax: 0521- 8 61 15

**WILLY GILTMANN – CLAUS DIERCKS 202**
ART & WERBETEAM GMBH
Borselstrasse 3
2000 Hamburg 50
Tel. 040-390 79 72/73/74
Fax: 040-390 79 75

**HILBEL, VOLKER 203**
Kronwinklerstrasse 24
8000 München 60
Tel. 089-863 24 22
Fax: 089-863 24 71

**HURLEBAUS, UWE 200-201**
Gaildorfer Strasse 80
7157 Murrhardt 2
Tel. 07192-5155
Fax: 07192-1666

Agent:
GUDRUN TEMPELMANN-BOEHR
Am Rosenbaum 7
4006 Erkrath
Tel. 0211-25 46 32

**KOREJWO, URSZULA 195**
Borstellstrasse 36
1000 Berlin 41
Tel. 030-219 000 72
Fax: 030-219 000 71

**MAIER, ALBERT-ERICH 198**
Mühlgasse 8
7959 Unterbalzheim
Tel. 07347-7165
Fax: 07347-7919

**MOOS-DREVENSTEDT, ERIKA 193**
Paul-Gerhardt-Strasse 23
4156 Willich 2 – Anrath
Tel. 02156-3806
Fax: 02156-1380

**PLIKAT, ARI 194**
Steinmetzstrasse 13
4600 Dortmund
Tel. 0231-51 52 27
Fax: 0231-51 59 17

Represented by:
GUDRUN TEMPELMANN-BOEHR
Am Rosenbaum 7
4006 Erkrath 1
Tel. 0211-25 32 46
Fax: 0211-25 46 32

**RINKE, VOLKMAR 190**
Albertus-Magnus-Strasse 55
3200 Hildesheim
Tel. 05121-26 30 10

**ROCHE, ANDRÉ 199**
Katharinenstrasse 10
8000 München 71
Tel. 089- 79 50 15
Fax: 089-791 78 59

**TECHNICAL ART GmbH 191**
NORBERT SCHÄFER
LUDWIG EBERL
Dreieichstrasse 50
6057 Dietzenbach
Tel. 06074-25033
25081
Fax: 06074-25033

**WIND, SIGI 204**
Eichendorffstrasse 43
8012 Ottobrunn
Tel. 089-609 04 61
Fax: 089-609 05 62

**WOHLGEMUTH, STEPHAN 197**
Steinlestrasse 32
6000 Frankfurt 70
Tel. 069-631 38 72

# Holland
# Hollande
# Holland

**7 ARTS STUDIOS BV 214-215**
Wilhelminapark 114
5041 EG Tilburg
Tel. 013-43 27 83
35 53 41
Fax: 013-42 76 45

**VAN DER LOO, FRANKA 212**
Binnenkadijk 322
1018 AZ Amsterdam
Tel. 020-23 36 89

**WIERSMA, JURGEN 216**
Weth. Frankeweg 26
1098 LA Amsterdam
Tel. 020-92 86 10
Fax: 020-92 86 10

Agents:
THE ARTBOX
Kruislaan 182
1098 SK Amsterdam
Tel. 020-668 15 51
Fax: 020- 93 99 07

STEVEN WELLS
ILLUSTRATION AGENCY
P.O. Box 651
London SE25 5PS
Tel. 081-689 1427
Fax: 081-683 0607

# Hong Kong
# Hongkong
# Hong Kong

**CHEONG, LUK WAI 94-95**
3306 Ka Wing House
Ka Tin Court
New Territories
Hong Kong
Tel. 697 65 45
Fax: +852-602 09 83

**CHEUNG CHI KWONG, ERIC 99**
No. A2 7/F Paramount Mansion
389 Chatham Road North
Kowloon
Hong Kong
Tel. 364 18 36
Pager: 116 89 23 A/C 8229

**LENEVEU, HELENE 98**
2 Robinson Road, 6/F
Mid Levels
Hong Kong
Tel. 858 85 29

**MEKISIC, ZORAN 96-97**
Z ART
4/F, Flat E, 17 Chi Fu Road
Chi Fu
Hong Kong
Tel. 551 94 07
Fax: 551 94 07
Pager: 116 88 99 Call 2886

**INDEX TO ADVERTISER**

**REGENT PUBLISHING SERVICES LTD. 16**
Hong Kong Office:
Call George Tai
REGENT PUBLISHING SERVICES LTD.
24th Floor, Federal Centre
77 Sheung On Street
Chai Wan
Hong Kong
Tel. 852-897 78 03
Fax: 852-558 72 09

New York Office:
Call Albert Yokum
REGENT PUBLISHING SERVICES LTD.
127 East 59th Street
New York, NY 10022, USA
Tel. 212-371 4506
Fax: 212-371 4609

London Office:
Call Gordon Beckwith
REGENT PUBLISHING SERVICES LTD.
4th Floor, 4 Brandon Road
London N7 9TP, UK
Tel. 071-607 3322
Fax: 071-700 4985

# Italy
# Italie
# Italien

**BARTOLI, GIULIANO 219**
Via Conchetta, 9
20136 Milano
Tel. 02-832 93 11
New No. 02-894 073 95

**BATTESTA, FABRIZIO 220**
Via Spalti, 18
30026 Portogruaro (Venezia)
Tel. 0421-7 50 04
Fax: 0421-7 50 04

**BORNIA-MONTICELLI 221**
Via Coni Zugna, 7
20021 Bollate (Milano)
Tel. 02-661 019 29
351 28 17

**CAMERINI, DANA 222**
Corso Italia, 42
20122 Milano
Tel. 02-894 022 74
New No. 02-583 113 67

**CAUDURO, FIORELLA 223**
Borgo Tegolaio, 17
50125 Firenze
Tel. 055-21 52 04

**COSTA, GIAMPIETRO 224**
Via Calderara, 5
37138 Verona
Tel. 045-57 78 33
Fax: 045-57 78 33

Agent:
MILAN ILLUSTRATIONS AGENCY
Via G. Parini, 12
20121 Milano
Tel. 02-290 026 32
Fax: 02-657 24 85

**D'ALTAN, PAOLO 225**
Via Vigevano, 27
20144 Milano
Tel. 02-832 18 68

**ELLI, PAOLA PATRIZIA 219**
Via Conchetta, 9
20136 Milano
Tel. 02-832 93 11
New No. 02-894 073 95

**FUZELLIER, MICHEL 226**
Via S. Nicolao, 10
20123 Milano
Tel. 02-80 02 94
Fax: 02-80 76 60

**GATTO, PIERLUIGI 227**
Via Inama, 3
20133 Milano
Tel. 02-74 48 37

**GUZZONI, RODOLFO 228**
Via Correggio, 14
20149 Milano
Tel. 02-49 13 52

## Italy
## Italie
## Italien

**RE, MARIASTEFANIA 229**
Via Correggio, 14
20149 Milano
Tel. 02-49 13 52

**RIBOLI, STEFANO 230**
Via Perola, 2/B
24021 Albino (Bergamo)
Tel. 035-75 46 07
Fax: 035-75 46 07

**ROSA, GUIDO 232**
Via Landoni, 9
28100 Novara
Tel. 0321-40 21 46
Fax: 0321-40 21 46

**ROSSINO, MICHELANGELO 231**
Via S. Quintino, 23
10121 Torino
Tel. 011-54 90 63

**SCANDELLA, ALESSANDRA 234**
Via Tantardini, 1/A
20136 Milano
Tel. 02-894 060 90

**SODANO, FRANCO 233**
Via Degli Orti, 9
22054 Mandello Del Lario (Como)
Tel. 0341-73 02 91

**VALLE, GIAN CARLO 235**
Via Bionaz, 7
10142 Torino
Tel. 011-707 22 79

## Japan
## Japon
## Japan

**ABE, MARIKO 102-103**
STAFF ILLUSTRATION JIGYOBU
Shinwa Building
2-9-2 Nishitenma
Kita-ku
Osaka 530
Tel. 06-363 4963
Fax: 06-363 4937

**ARAI, MASATO 104**
8-9-6 Shakujii-cho
Nerima-ku
Tokyo 177
Tel. 03-3996 0676
Fax: 03-3996 0676

**EGUCHI, SHUHEI 106-107**
5-B Kyoritsukosan Shiroganedai Bldg.
5-3-3 Shiroganedai
Minato-ku
Tokyo 108
Tel. 03-3473 8423

**FUJIKAKE, CHARLOTTE 108**
702 Ars Nakameguro
1-3-3 Higashiyama
Meguro-ku
Tokyo 153
Tel. 03-3719 1244

**FUJIKAKE, MASAKUNI 109**
702 Ars Nakameguro
1-3-3 Higashiyama
Meguro-ku
Tokyo 153
Tel. 03-3719 1244

**FUJIWARA, HIROYUKI 110-111**
301 Corpo Nemu
2-11-3 Takada No Baba
Shinjuku-ku
Tokyo 169
Tel. 03-3232 0843
Fax: 03-3208 2449

**FURUTA, TADAO 105**
503 Denken Kyodo Dai-1 Mansion
5-33-3 Kyodo
Setagaya-ku
Tokyo 156
Tel. 03-3426 2819

**HAKAMADA, KAZUO 112**
6-13-15-406 Toyotama Kita
Nerima-ku
Tokyo 176
Tel. 03-5999 2383
Fax: 03-5999 2383

Agent:
POINT DELTA & ATY GROUP, INC.
Yasuhisa Azuma
295 Madison Ave., Suite #926
New York, NY 10017
Tel. 212-949 7639
Fax: 212-949 7633

**HIRANO, KEIKO 113**
301 An House Kaminoge
1-25-13 Kaminoge
Setagaya-ku
Tokyo 158
Tel. 03-5706 6548

**IGAWA, HIDEO 114**
3-A, Arubosu
5-31-17 Okusawa
Setagaya-ku
Tokyo 158
Tel. 03-3722 6479

**ITAGAKI, SHUN 115**
5-16-10-402 Minami Azabu
Minato-ku
Tokyo 106
Tel. 03-3446 8300

**KANNO, KENICHI 116**
203 Yoyogi Panbial Building
1-2-4 Tomigaya
Shibuya-ku
Tokyo 151
Tel. 03-3467 9484

**KAWADA, HISAO 117**
1001 Nisho Iwai Honancho Mansion
1-51-7 Honan
Suginami-ku
Tokyo 168
Tel. 03-3328 8906

**KAWAMURA, OSAMU 118**
302 Harajuku Jitorunku
4-15-16 Jingumae
Shibuya-ku
Tokyo 150
Tel. 03-3403 3343

**KAWARASAKI, HIDEYUKI 119**
5-6-6-403 Tsurukawa
Machida City
Tokyo 194-01
Tel. 0427-34 4677

**MORI, SADAHITO 120-121**
55-3 Wakakusa-cho
Minami-ku
Nagoya City
Aichi 457
Tel. 052-823 2909

**NAGINO, TAKAHIRO 122**
401 Le Soleil
2-3-4 Sendagaya
Shibuya-ku
Tokyo 151
Tel. 03-3479 6975
Fax: 03-3408 2478

**NAKAJIMA, HIDE 123**
STAFF, INC.
410-8 Kameino
Fujisawa City
Kanagawa 252
Tel. 0466-82 9638
Fax: 0466-82 9638

**OGAWA, KAZUMI 124**
101 Arusu Zama Tatsunodai
75-1 Tatsunodai
Zama City
Kanagawa 228
Tel. 0462-57 2477
Fax: 0462-57 2478

**OKUDA, TAKAAKI 125**
203 Berubyu Musashino
3-10-13 Nishiogi Kita
Suginami-ku
Tokyo 167
Tel. 03-3301 9659

**SAKAI, HARECHIKA 126-127**
986-6 Ooeda
Kasukabe City
Saitama 344
Tel. 048-736 9845

**SATO, TOYOHIKO 128-129**
STUDIO SUPER, INC.
1-43-23-303 Tomigaya
Shibuya-ku
Tokyo 151
Tel. 03-3468 1657

**SEKINE, TATSUMI 130**
206 Green Park Kawasaki
3-1-3 Fujisaki
Kawasaki-ku
Kawasaki City
Kanagawa 210
Tel. 044-266 6110

**SHELLEY, JOHN 131**
501-3-18-12 Shiroganedai
Minato-ku
Tokyo 108
Tel. 03-3443 8949
Fax: 03-3444 3198

18 Spinney Road
Thorpe St. Andrew Norwich
Norfolk NR7 0PW
United Kingdom
Tel. 0603-31585

**SHIBATA, HITOSHI 132-133**
202 Jochi House
1-1-24 Hiroo
Shibuya-ku
Tokyo 150
Tel. 03-3499 1637

**SHIOYA, HIROAKI 134**
201 Frorie Hosoyama
751 Shinmaruko-cho
Nakahara-ku
Kawasaki City
Kanagawa 211
Tel. 044-733 3731
Fax: 044-733 3731

Agent:
POINT DELTA & ATY GROUP, INC.
Yasuhisa Azuma
295 Madison Ave., Suite #926
New York, NY 10017
Tel. 212-949 7639
Fax: 212-949 7633

**TAKAHASHI, KINTARO 135**
103 Chatelet Blanche
12-35 Sarugaku-cho
Shibuya-ku
Tokyo 150
Tel. 03-3476 2314

**TAKAUJI, MASAAKI 136-137**
1007 Nakano Dai-2 Corpo
5-24-16 Nakano
Nakano-ku
Tokyo 164
Tel. 03-3228 6889

**TOMISAWA, TEN 138**
3-84 Mukaikogane
Nagareyama City
Chiba 270-01
Tel. 0471-75 2282

**TSUKUSHI 139**
305 Palaision Asagaya
1-6-7 Asagaya Minami
Suginami-ku
Tokyo 166
Tel. 03-3315 4592

**WATANABE, FUMIO 140**
804 Konte Nishikasai
3-8-7 Nishikasai
Edogawa-ku
Tokyo 134
Tel. 03-3675 8526

## Korea
## Corée
## Korea

**CROSS CULTURAL CENTER FOR ASIA 142-143**
Hosan Building, 2F
709-8, Banpo-Dong
Seocho-ku
Seoul 137 040
Tel. 02-512 3948
512 3949
Fax: 02-512 3948

**HANIL DESIGN 145**
Dae Sung Building #502
48-4, Choongmooro, 2 Ga
Joong-gu
Seoul
Tel. 02-266 5140
275 7410

**HART WORK / HUH SANG-HOE 146-147**
Zip 100-271
Room No. 502 Dongwha Building
43-1 Pil-Dong, 1-Ga
1, Chung-gu
Seoul
Tel. 02-272 6971

**ILLUSTBANK 152-153**
Sang-A Building
2133 Bang Bae-Dong
Seocho-Gu
Seoul 137 069
Tel. 02-591 8463
591 7565
Fax: 02-591 7565

**KANG, WOO-HYON 148**
Agent:
CROSS CULTURAL CENTER FOR ASIA
Hosan Building, 2F
709-8, Banpo-Dong
Seocho-ku
Seoul 137 040
Tel. 02-512 3948
512 3949
Fax: 02-512 3948

**KIM, EUN-JOO 149**

**LEE, BOK-SHIK 150**
160, Kil-Dong
Kang Dong-ku
Seoul
Tel. 02-485 6385

**LEE, HEARY 151**
17-25 Sibum Apt.
Yeoido-Dong
Youngdungpo-gu
Seoul
Tel. 02-782 4147

**LEE, JOON-SUP 155**
330-36, Sukyo-Dong
Mapo-ku
Seoul
Tel. 02-337 0360

**LEE, SUNG-PYO 157**
407-1407, Chugong Apt.
Kwachon
Kyongki-do
Tel. 02-502 9607

**LIU, JAE-SOO 156**
Hosan Building, 2F
709-8, Banpo-Dong
Seocho-ku
Seoul 137 040
Tel. 02-512 3948
512 3949
543 9853
Fax: 02-512 3948

**OUK, KANG-CHANG 158**
254-10, Shin Hun Dong
Seo-gu
In Chun
Tel. 032-572 1915

**RHIE, WON-BOK 159**
Song-pa
Shinchun 7
Jangmi A. 14-1407
Seoul 134 240
Tel. 02-422 1256

## Malaysia
## Malaisie
## Malaysia

**CREATIVE ENTERPRISE SDN. BHD. 163-167**
38 Jalan 1/82B
Bangsar Utama
59000 Kuala Lumpur
Tel. 03-230 49 70
Fax: 03-230 49 67

**TAIB, JAAFAR 163**
CREATIVE ENTERPRISE SDN. BHD.

**HUSSEIN, ZAINAL BUANG 164**
CREATIVE ENTERPRISE SDN. BHD.

**YUSOF, AZMAN 165**
CREATIVE ENTERPRISE SDN. BHD.

## Norway
## Norvège
## Norwegen

**DÉVILLE DESIGN A/S 239**
Parkveien 62A
0254 Oslo 2
Tel. 02-44 24 80
Fax: 02-55 18 20

## Portugal
## Portugal
## Portugal

**CAMPOS, PEDRO 242**
Rua Heróis Dadra 2-1.º Dt.º
Damaia
2700 Amadora
Tel. 97 05 59
97 24 39
Fax: 67 84 89

**SILVA, JORGE 243**
Est. Benfica, 584 1.º Dt.º
1500 Lisboa
Tel. 716 39 49

## Spain
## Espagne
## Spanien

**ALVAREZ, LUIS 246**
Santa Perpetua, 14 Ent.
08012 Barcelona
Tel. 93-218 62 10
Fax: 93-218 62 10

**AMECHAZURRA, GERARDO 264**
Representado en exclusiva por
GOLD-2
Dr. Fleming, 26
28036 Madrid
Tel. 91-457 73 97
Fax: 91-563 49 99

**CIFANI, DANIEL 262**
Calle del Pez, 12-1.º G
28004 Madrid
Tel. 91-522 77 34

**DE PEDRO, BEATRIZ 257**
Calle Cartagena, 131-5.º Izq.
28002 Madrid
Tel. 91-564 35 60

**DIAZ SANTANA, HUMBERTO 252-253**
Victor Andrés Belaúnde, 9-2.º Izq.
28016 Madrid
Tel. 91-430 57 54
Fax: 91-430 57 54

**FCO. PÉREZ FRUTOS (FRAN) 259**
Jaén, 11 - Bajo E
28020 Madrid
Tel. 91-535 35 84
656 08 94

**FLORES, MIGUEL ANGEL 260**
Avenida de Francia, 24-3.º C
28916 Leganes (Madrid)
Tel. 91-686 45 88

**GAMERO, PEDRO 258**
Av. del Doctor García Tapia 110, 8.º B
28030 Madrid
Tel. 91-437 33 13

**GIL, MIGUEL A. / GIL, GUSTAVO 267**
Pº Castellana, 266-5.º C
Madrid
Tel. 91-314 76 35

**GONZALEZ TEJA, RAMÓN 256**
Cartagena 16-5.º C
28028 Madrid
Tel. 91-245 14 43
Fax: 91-245 14 43

**IRÚN, ANTONIO 263**
Representado en España por
GOLD-2
Dr. Fleming, 26
28036 Madrid
Tel. 91-457 73 97
Fax: 91-563 49 99

**LERIA, SANTIAGO 251**
Gran Via, 80, 2.º
28013 Madrid
Tel. 91-247 22 51
247 76 00 (Ext. 48)
Fax: 91-247 22 51

**OVILO, MANUEL 265**
Calle Datil N.º 13
28025 Madrid
Tel. 91-711 56 10
462 11 83

**MISTIANO, MAURO 254**
General Alvarez de Castro, 43
Bajo Derecha
28010 Madrid
Tel. 91-445 07 77
Fax: 91-445 07 77

**MOGICA, TEO 261**
Marroquina, 106-7.º B
28030 Madrid
Tel. 91-439 87 95

**RAMOS, EUGENIO 248**
Plaza Olavide, 5
28010 Madrid
Tel. 91-448 24 04
Fax: 91-448 51 46

**RIGAU, JOAN 250**
Avenida Coll del Portell, 59B
08024 Barcelona
Tel. 93-210 69 08

**ROCAROLS, ALBERT 249**
Rosellón, 148-5.º 2.ª
08036 Barcelona
Tel. 93-454 29 71

Represented in USA by:
S.I. International – HERB SPIERS
43 East 19th Street
New York, NY 10003
Tel. 212-254 4996
Fax: 212-995 0911

**ROURA, ENRIQUE 266**
Calle Joaquín Costa, 51
28002 Madrid
Tel. 91-563 99 02

**TRAVIESO, MIGUEL 247**
Plaza de la Cruz, 3
47162 Aldeamayor de S. Martin
(Valladolid)
Tel. 983-55 69 51

**XARRIE, JUAN 255**
Calle Gloria, 3
28820 Coslada (Madrid)
Tel. 91-673 76 72
Fax: 91-673 86 29

**INDEX TO ADVERTISER**

**COMERCIAL ATHENEUM, S.A. 268**
Consejo de Ciento, 130-136
08015 Barcelona
Tel. 93-423 14 51 / 52 / 53
Fax: 93-426 84 04

Rufino González, 26
28037 Madrid
Tel. 91-754 20 62
Fax: 91-754 09 02

## Switzerland
## Suisse
## Schweiz

**CLAUSON, THIERRY 206-207**
Rue des Eaux-Vives 27
1207 Genève
Tel. 022-736 65 10
Fax: 022-736 65 10

**WILLIS, JULIAN 208**
Route de Vaulion 18
1323 Romainmôtier
Tel. 024-53 16 32
Fax: 024-53 16 32

## United Kingdom
## Grande-Bretagne
## Grossbritannien

**ARTISTS INC. LTD 280**
7-8 Rathbone Place
London W1P 1DE
Tel. 071-580 6642
Fax: 071-436 5183

**CHAMBERLAIN, JOHN 271**
14 Telston Close
Bourne End
Bucks. SL8 5TY
Tel. 06285-21941

**ECKFORD, RICHARD GRAHAM 274**
Stickleys Barn Minchington
Near Blandford
Dorset DT11 8DH
Tel. 0725-516 320

**GUTTERIDGE, DUNCAN 272**
15 Wokindon Road
Chadwell–St. Mary
Grays
Essex RM16 4QT
Tel. 03752-3867
Fax: 03752-6169

**INDUSTRIAL ART STUDIO 277**
ROGER FULL
Consols, St. Ives
Cornwall TR26 2HW
Tel. 0736-797651
Fax: 0736-794291

INDUSTRIAL ART STUDIO
Hornsteinstrasse 18
D–8000 München 80
Tel. 089-982 82 82
Fax: 089- 98 11 66

**JONES, STEVE 273**
THE PORTFOLIO GALLERY
22 Bangor Street
Port Dinorwic
Gwynedd LL56 4JD
Tel. 0248-671459

**LAWRENCE, JOHN 278**
Lower Oakshott Farmhouse
Hawkley, Liss
Hants. GU33 6LP
Tel. 073-084220
Fax: 073-084246

**MEACHEM, LESTER 283**
73 Mount Pleasant Lane
London E5 9EW
Tel. 081-806 5449

**OUTLOOK CREATIVE SERVICES LTD. 279**
KENNY McARTHUR
25 Bruton Place
London W1X 7AB
Tel. 071-499 2610
Fax: 071-355 3761

**PHILLIPS, ARTHUR 276**
16 Broomfield Road
Surbiton
Surrey KT5 9AZ
Tel. 081-399 5835 (home)
081-547 3299 (studio)
Fax: 081-541 3732

**SMITH, GRAHAM 275**
57 Rothschild Road
Chiswick
London W4 5NT
Tel. 081-994 6115

**SOBR, PENNY 284**
Flat 4
149 Holland Park Avenue
London W11 4UX
Tel. 071-371 6809

Studio address:
PARTNERSHIP STUDIO
9 Macklin Street
London WC2B 5NH
Tel. 071-404 8265

**THOMPSON, GARY 281**
Flat 5
47 Ventnor Villas
Hove
East Sussex BN3 3DB
Tel. 0273-204196

**TILL, DAVID 282**
94 Park Avenue South
London N8 8LS
Tel. 081-348 9012

## United States
## Etats-Unis
## Vereinigte Staaten

**ABE, GEORGE 18**
Represented by:
KOLEA BAKER
Pier 70 – 2815 Alaskan Way
Seattle, Washington 98131
Tel. 206-443 0326

**ANSLEY, FRANK 25**
Represented by:
COREY GRAHAM
Pier 33 North
San Francisco, California 94111
Tel. 415-956 4750

**BAKER, DON 19**
Represented by:
KOLEA BAKER
Pier 70 – 2815 Alaskan Way
Seattle, Washington 98131
Tel. 206-443 0326

**BAKER, KOLEA 18-21**
Pier 70 – 2815 Alaskan Way
Seattle, Washington 98131
Tel. 206-443 0326

**BOIES, ALEX 50**
Represented by:
JERRY LEFF ASSOC.
420 Lexington Avenue
New York, NY 10170
Tel. 212-697 8525

**BRICE, JEFF 20**
Represented by:
KOLEA BAKER
Pier 70 – 2815 Alaskan Way
Seattle, Washington 98131
Tel. 206-443 0326

**BRONCATO, RON 46**
Represented by:
LINDA JAGOW
PO Box 425
Rochester, NY 14604
Tel. 716-546 7606

**CEBALLOS, JOHN 39**
Represented by:
SCOTT HULL ASSOCIATES
68 East Franklin Street
Rayton, Ohio 45459
Tel. 513-433 8383

**CHAN, RON 56**
Represented by:
JIM LILIE
251 Kearny Street
San Francisco, California 94108
Tel. 415-441 4384

**CONGE, BOB 47**
Represented by:
LINDA JAGOW
PO Box 425
Rochester, NY 14604
Tel. 716-546 7606

**CSICSKO, DAVID 23**
Represented by:
RANDI FIAT & ASSOC.
612 North Michigan Avenue
Chicago, Illinois 60611
Tel. 312-664 8322

# United States
# Etats-Unis
# Vereinigte Staaten

**DENHAM, KARL 29**
155 Fifth Street
Hoboken, New Jersey 07030
Tel. 201-792 6422

**DICIANNI, RON 51**
Represented by:
JERRY LEFF ASSOC.
420 Lexington Avenue
New York, NY 10170
Tel. 212-697 8525

**DOTY, ELDON 36**
Represented by:
HK PORTFOLIO
458 Newton Turnpike
Weston, Connecticut 06883
Tel. 203-545 4687

**RANDI FIAT & ASSOC. 22-23**
612 North Michigan Avenue
Chicago, Illinois 60611
Tel. 312-664 8322

**GOLDBERG, RICHARD 30-31**
368 Congress Street
Boston, Massachusetts 02110
Tel. 617-338 6369

**GOLDMAN, DAVID 32-33**
41 Union Square West #918
New York, NY 10003
Tel. 212-807 6627

**GRAHAM, COREY 25-28**
Pier 33 North
San Francisco, California 94111
Tel. 415-956 4750

**GRETCHEN HARRIS ASSOC. 42-44**
5230 13th Avenue South
Minneapolis, Michigan 55417
Tel. 612-822 0650

**HENRIE, CARY 34-35**
310 East 46th Street #5H
New York, NY 10017
Tel. 212-986 0299

**HK PORTFOLIO 36-37**
458 Newton Turnpike
Weston, Connecticut 06883
Tel. 203-545 4687

**SCOTT HULL ASSOCIATES 38-41**
68 East Franklin Street
Rayton, Ohio 45459
Tel. 513-433 8383

**JACKSON, LANCE / SYNTAX 45**
1790 5th Street
Berkeley, California 94710
Tel. 415-849 0560

**JACOBSEN, KEN 43**
Represented by:
GRETCHEN HARRIS ASSOC.
5230 13th Avenue South
Minneapolis, Michigan 55417
Tel. 612-822 0650

**JAGOW, LINDA 46-47**
PO Box 425
Rochester, NY 14604
Tel. 716-546 7606

**JARVIS, NATHAN Y. 44**
Represented by:
GRETCHEN HARRIS ASSOC.
5230 13th Avenue South
Minneapolis, Michigan 55417
Tel. 612-822 0650

**KLEBER, JOHN 22**
Represented by:
RANDI FIAT & ASSOC.
612 North Michigan Avenue
Chicago, Illinois 60611
Tel. 312-664 8322

**JERRY LEFF ASSOC. 48-51**
420 Lexington Avenue
New York, NY 10170
Tel. 212-697 8525

**LESTER, MIKE 52-53**
8890 River Terrace Drive
Duluth, Georgia 30136
Tel. 447 5332

**LILIE, JIM 54-59**
251 Kearny Street
San Francisco, California 94108
Tel. 415-441 4384

**LIVINGSTON, FRANCIS 48**
Represented by:
JERRY LEFF ASSOC.
420 Lexington Avenue
New York, NY 10070
Tel. 212-697 8525

**LŌSE, HAL 60**
533 W. Hortter Street
Philadelphia, Pennsylvania
Tel. 215-849 7635

**MAGOVERN, PEG 26**
Represented by:
COREY GRAHAM
Pier 33 North
San Francisco, California 94111
Tel. 415-956 4750

**MAHONEY, PATRICIA 27**
Represented by:
COREY GRAHAM
Pier 33 North
San Francisco, California 94111
Tel. 415-956 4750

**MANNING, MICHELE 49**
Represented by:
JERRY LEFF ASSOC.
420 Lexington Avenue
New York, NY 10070
Tel. 212-697 8525

**MARSHALL, CRAIG 59**
Represented by:
JIM LILIE
251 Kearny Street
San Francisco, California 94108
Tel. 415-441 4384

**MURRAY, JOHN 61**
337 Summer Street
Boston, Massachusetts 02210
Tel. 617-426 0359

**NACHT, MERLE 62**
374 Main Street
Wethersfield, Connecticut 06109
Tel. 203-563 7993

**NAKAMURA, JOEL 28**
Represented by:
COREY GRAHAM
Pier 33 North
San Francisco, California 94111
Tel. 415-956 4750

**PECHANEC, VLADIMIR 63**
34-43 Crescent Street
Long Island City, NY 11106
Tel. 718-729 3973

**PITTS, TED 40**
Represented by:
SCOTT HULL ASSOCIATES
68 East Franklin Street
Rayton, Ohio 45459
Tel. 513-433 8383

**RENFRO, EDWARD 64**
250 East 83rd Street #4E
New York, NY 10028
Tel. 212-879 3823

**RIEDY, MARK 38**
Represented by:
SCOTT HULL ASSOCIATES
68 East Franklin Street
Rayton, Ohio 45459
Tel. 513-433 8383

**RODA, BOT 65**
78 Victoria Lane
Lancaster, Pennsylvania 17603
Tel. 717-393 1406

**ROWND, JIM 42**
Represented by:
GRETCHEN HARRIS ASSOC.
5230 13th Avenue South
Minneapolis, Michigan 55417
Tel. 612-822 0650

**SHARP, BRUCE 21**
Represented by:
KOLEA BAKER
Pier 70
2815 Alaskan Way
Seattle, Washington 98131
Tel. 206-443 0326

**SHAW, KURT 67**
2954 Sheraden Boulevard
Pittsburg, Pennsylvania 15204
Tel. 412-771 7345

**SEAVER, JEFF 66**
130 West 24th Street
New York, NY 10011
Tel. 212-741 2279

**SIRREL, TERRY 72**
768 Red Oak Drive
Bartlett, Illinois
Tel. 708-213 9003

**SPOSATO, JOHN 68-69**
43 East 22nd Street #2A
New York, NY 10010
Tel. 212-477 3909

**STERMER, DUGALD 55**
Represented by:
JIM LILIE
251 Kearny Street
San Francisco, California 94108
Tel. 415-441 4384

**TUCKER, EZRA 57**
Represented by:
JIM LILIE
251 Kearny Street
San Francisco, California 94108
Tel. 415-441 4384

**VANDERBEEK, DON 41**
Represented by:
SCOTT HULL ASSOCIATES
68 East Franklin Street
Rayton, Ohio 45459
Tel. 513-433 8383

**VERNAGLIA, MICHAEL 70-71**
1251 Bloomfield Street
Hoboken, New Jersey 07030
Tel. 201-792 4994

**VEROUGSTRAETE, RANDY 37**
Represented by:
HK PORTFOLIO
458 Newton Turnpike
Weston, Connecticut 06883
Tel. 203-545 4687

**WATTS, STAN 58**
Represented by:
JIM LILIE
251 Kearny Street
San Francisco, California 94108
Tel. 415-441 4384

**WORCESTER, MARY 42**
Represented by:
GRETCHEN HARRIS ASSOC.
5230 13th Avenue South
Minneapolis, Michigan 55417
Tel. 612-822 0650

**ZIMINSKY, DENNIS 54**
Represented by:
JIM LILIE
251 Kearny Street
San Francisco, California 94108
Tel. 415-441 4384

The Spirit of America
A STATE-BY-STATE CELEBRATION
CHARLES MATHES
Introduction by Bob Hope
Scotch and Water
ISLAY · JURA · MULL · SKYE
Neil Wilson

# Illustrators

## United States
## Etats-Unis
## Vereinigte Staaten

The following American illustration pages have been made possible through collaboration with American Showcase.

# G E O R G E ◆ A B E

◆ Kolea Baker • Artist Representative • 2819 First Avenue Suite 240 • Seattle , Washington 98121 • 206 . 443 . 0326 • Fax 206 . 448 . 4219

# D O N ◆ B A K E R

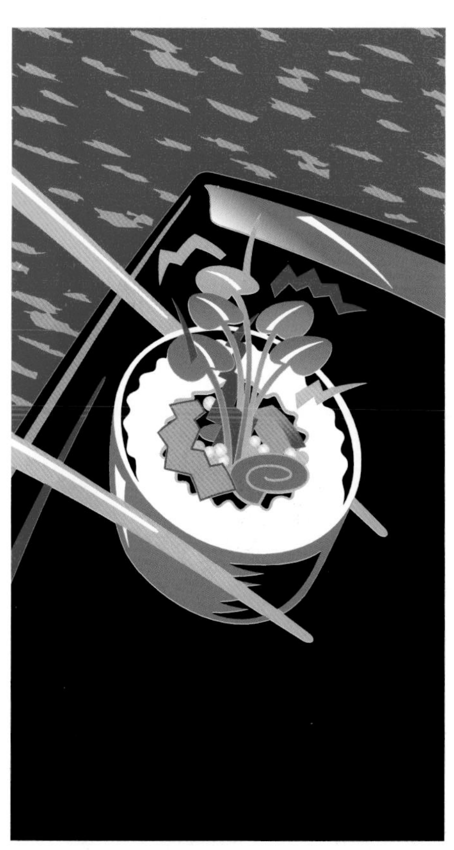

◆ Kolea Baker • Artist Representative • 2819 First Avenue Suite 240 • Seattle , Washington 98121 • 206 . 443 . 0326 • Fax 206 . 448 . 4219

# J E F F ◆ B R I C E

◆ Kolea Baker ◆ Artist Representative ◆ 2819 First Avenue Suite 240 ◆ Seattle, Washington 98121 ◆ 206 . 443 . 0326 ◆ Fax 206 . 448 . 4219

# B R U C E ◆ S H A R P

◆ Kolea Baker • Artist Representative • 2819 First Avenue Suite 240 • Seattle , Washington 98121 • 206 . 443 . 0326 • Fax 206 . 448 . 4219

# JOHNKLEBER


Randi Fiat & Associates
612 North Michigan Avenue
Chicago, IL 60611
312.664.8322
FAX 312.7879486

Martha Productions
4445 Overland Avenue
Culver City, CA 90230
213.204.1771
FAX 213.204.4598

Kurt Grubaugh
Artist Representative
1239 Waterview Drive
Mill Valley, CA 94941
415.381.3038

John Kleber
ACME studios
314 5th Ave. South
Minneapolis, MN 55415
612.339.4222

ART DIRECTOR: DAVID SYREK AGENCY: CHICAGO TRIBUNE CLIENT: CHICAGO TRIBUNE

# DAVID CSICSKO

REPRESENTED BY RANDI FIAT AND ASSOCIATES TELEPHONE 312-664-8322 FAX 312-787-9486

**Frank Ansley/Illustration**

COREY GRAHAM
REPRESENTS
PIER 33 NORTH
SAN FRANCISCO
9 4 1 1 1
415 956 4750
FAX 391 6104

# peg **magovern**

COREY GRAHAM
REPRESENTS
PIER 33 NORTH
SAN FRANCISCO
9 4 1 1 1

415 956 4750
FAX 391 6104

See's
CANDIES

BonLait 70
CALORIES
fromage frais
Fat-Free
PEACH
Calcium-Fortified

**Joel Nakamura**
(818) 795-6460
FAX: (818) 577-6025

KaRL DeNHaM

155 Fifth Street Apt. C
Hoboken, NJ 07030
Phone 201 · 792 · 6422
Fax 201 · 792 · 0658

# *Global and Environmentally Safe*

**RICHARD A. GOLDBERG**

368 Congress Street, 5th Floor
Boston, MA 02210
(617) 338-6369
(617) 482-9062 FAX

Represented in New England by:
Deborah Lipman
506 Windsor Drive
Framingham, MA 01701
(508) 877-8830

# Global and Environmentally Safe

**RICHARD A. GOLDBERG**

368 Congress Street, 5th Floor
Boston, MA 02210
(617) 338-6369
(617) 482-9062 FAX

Represented in New England by:
Deborah Lipman
506 Windsor Drive
Framingham, MA 01701
(508) 877-8830

**David Goldman Agency**
41 Union Square West
Suite 918
New York, New York 10003
(212) 807-6627
FAX: (212) 463-8175

Representing:
**Norm Bendell**

Yes, we have an animation reel!

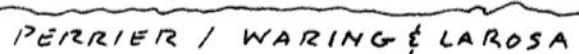

BUDGET GOURMET / DILORIO WERGELES

JOHNSON & JOHNSON / LINTAS

MELLON BANK / SAATCHI & SAATCHI

NATIONAL CAR RENTAL / CHIAT DAY MOJO

**David Goldman Agency**
41 Union Square West
Suite 918
New York, New York 10003
(212) 807-6627
FAX: (212) 463-8175

Representing:
**Norm Bendell**

Yes, we have an animation reel!

# *C*ary *H*enrie

310 EAST 46 STREET #5H, N.Y., N.Y. 10017 212 · 986 · 0299

*C*lients *I*nclude: TIME WARNER, AT&T, APPLE COMPUTER, LOTUS, SAMSUNG, MERRILL LYNCH, RJR NABISCO, NEW YORK LIFE, THE NEW YORK TIMES, BUSINESS WEEK, FORBES, ESQUIRE, SPORTS ILLUSTRATED, CONDÉ NAST TRAVELER, SCRIBNER'S, ST. MARTIN'S PRESS.

# Cary Henrie

310 EAST 46 STREET #5H, N.Y., N.Y. 10017 212 · 986 · 0299

*Clients Include:* TIME WARNER, AT&T, APPLE COMPUTER, LOTUS, SAMSUNG, MERRILL LYNCH, RJR NABISCO, NEW YORK LIFE, THE NEW YORK TIMES, BUSINESS WEEK, FORBES, ESQUIRE, SPORTS ILLUSTRATED, CONDÉ NAST TRAVELER, SCRIBNER'S, ST. MARTIN'S PRESS.

Contact Harriet Kasak
458 Newtown Turnpike
Weston, CT 06883
Telephone (203) 454-4687
Fax (203) 227-1366

# E L D O N  D O T Y

Contact Harriet Kasak
458 Newtown Turnpike
Weston, CT 06883
Telephone (203) 454-4687
Fax (203) 227-1366

# RANDY VEROUGSTRAETE

MARK RIEDY

Scott Hull Associates • FAX 513 433 0434 • NYC 212 966 3604 • 513 433 8383

# JOHN CEBALLOS

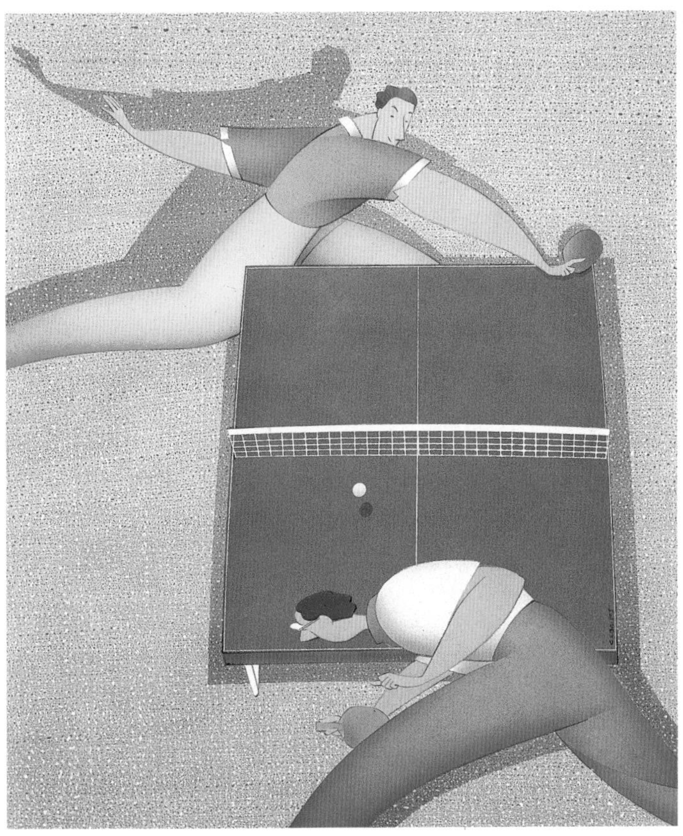

Scott Hull Associates • FAX 513 433 0434 • NYC 212 966 3604 • 513 433 8383

TED PITTS

Scott Hull Associates • FAX 513 433 0434 • NYC 212 966 3604 • 513 433 8383

# DON VANDERBEEK

Scott Hull Associates • FAX 513 433 0434 • NYC 212 966 3604 • 513 433 8383

## Jim Rownd

Represented by

Gretchen Harris

612/822-0650

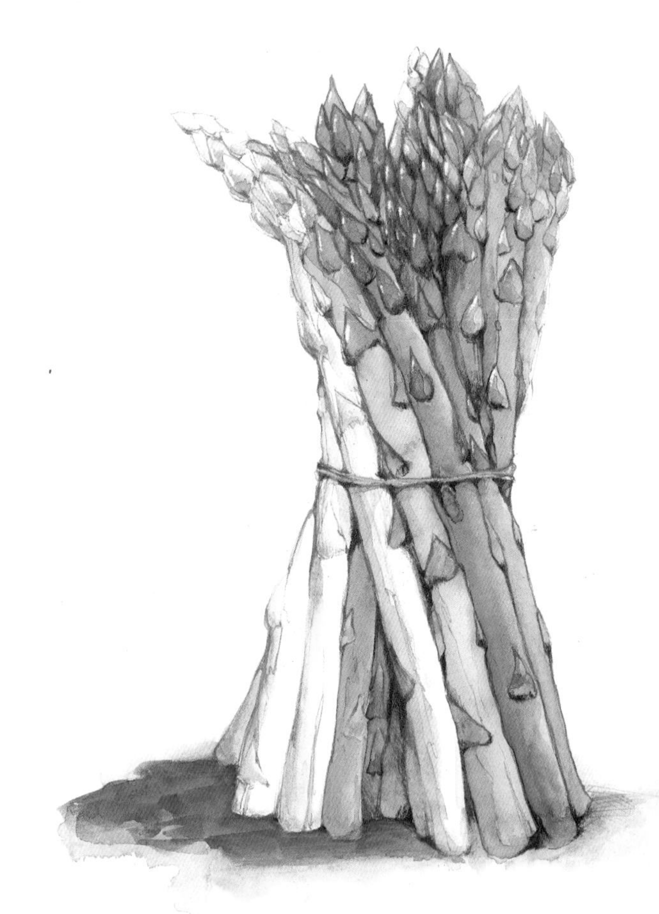

## Mary Worcester

Represented by

Gretchen Harris

612/822-0650

KEN JACOBSEN

ILLUSTRATION

IN MINNEAPOLIS CALL
GRETCHEN HARRIS 612 822 0650

IN SAN FRANCISCO CALL
KURT GRUBAUGH 415 381 3038

STUDIO

612 823 4662

# NATHAN Y. JARVIS

Nathan Y. Jarvis & Associates, Inc./Creative Services

*Close as a call.*
*Fast as a fax.*
*Always on time.*

To receive my promotional mailings, send your business card to
708a Main Street, Grandview, Missouri 64030-2329.
More of my work can be seen in the **CA**1990 Illustration Annual.

**Call NATHAN Y. JARVIS: 816-765-0617 Fax 765-8112**

*Represented in Minneapolis by Gretchen Harris & Associates 612 822-065*

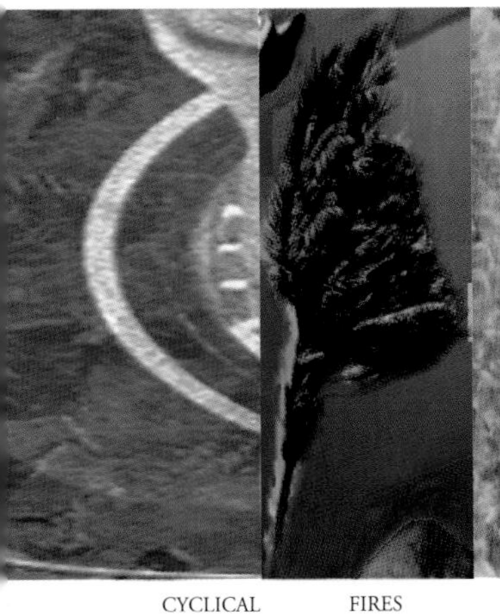

# LANCE JACKSON

Represented by
Syntax International

1790 Fifth Street
Berkeley, Ca. 94710
415.849.4313
Fax: 415.849.0574
MacNet: SyntaxDesign

Kyoto . New York . Paris

CYCLICAL FIRES

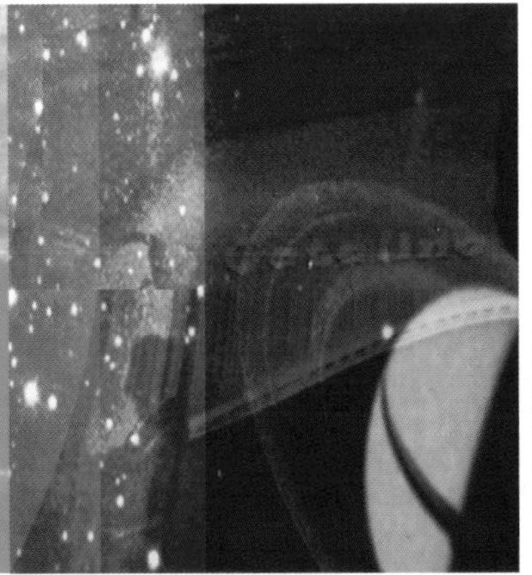

HEAVEN

SPEAK

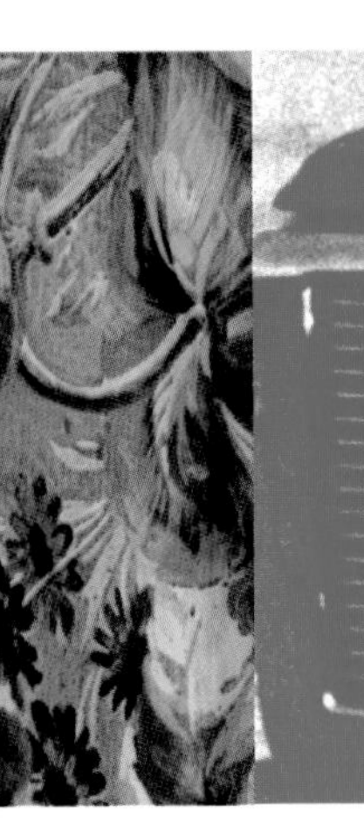

PLEASURE

HARDWARE

OMEN

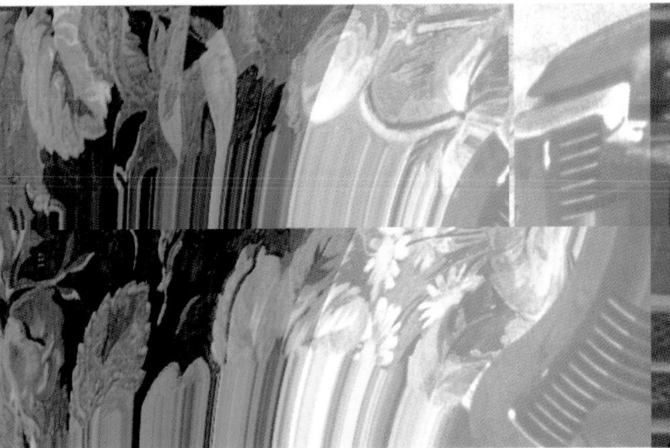

ASPARAGUS

YACHTING

HAPPY

# SYNTAX INTERNATIONAL

Represents
Lance Jackson

1790 Fifth Street
Berkeley, Ca. 94710
415.849.4313
Fax: 415.849.0574
MacNet: SyntaxDesign

Kyoto . New York . Paris

DINOSAUR

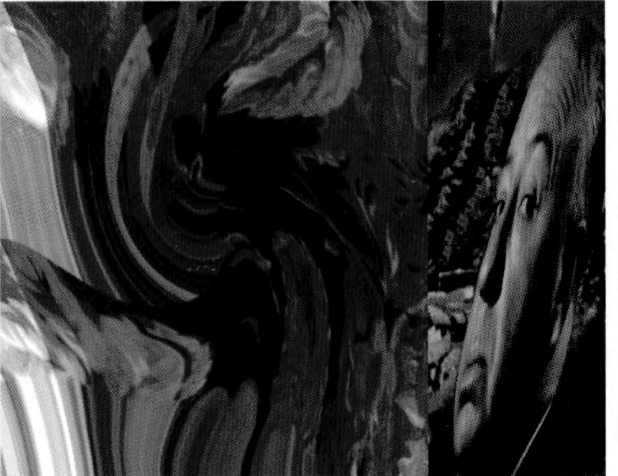

FRACTALS

VERTIGO

**Ron Brancato**
333 North Plymouth Avenue
Rochester, New York 14608
(716) 262-4450
FAX: (716) 262-3022

Represented in Western New York by
Linda Jagow/Illustrators Quorum
PO Box 425
Rochester, New York 14603
(716) 546-7606



Member: Type Directors Club/New York Illustrators Forum

Clients include: Agway, Citibank, DuPont, Kodak, Mobil, Remington, RIT, Xerox.

ROOT BROS.
Farms

Sales Information Guide

**Bob Conge**
28 Harper Street
Rochester, New York 14607
(716) 473-0291

In Tri-State Area:
Renard Represents
(212) 490-2450

"Netware LAN Drivers", Novell Inc.

# FRANCIS LIVINGSTON

REPRESENTED BY JERRY LEFF ASSOCIATES, INC. ■ 420 LEXINGTON AVE. ■ NEW YORK NY 10170 ■ TEL: 212-697-8525 ■ FAX: 212-949-1843

# MICHELE MANNING

REPRESENTED BY JERRY LEFF ASSOCIATES, INC. ■ 420 LEXINGTON AVE. ■ NEW YORK NY 10170 ■ TEL: 212-697-8525 ■ FAX: 212-949-1843

REPRESENTED BY JERRY LEFF ASSOCIATES, INC. ■ 420 LEXINGTON AVE. ■ NEW YORK NY 10170 ■ TEL: 212-697-8525 ■ FAX: 212-949-1843

## RON DICIANNI

REPRESENTED BY JERRY LEFF ASSOCIATES, INC. ■ 420 LEXINGTON AVE. ■ NEW YORK NY 10170 ■ TEL: 212-697-8525 ■ FAX: 212-949-1843

**Mike Lester**
(404) 447-5332
FAX: (404) 447-9559

MIKE LESTER

**Mike Lester**
(404) 447-5332
FAX: (404) 447-9559

MIKE LESTER

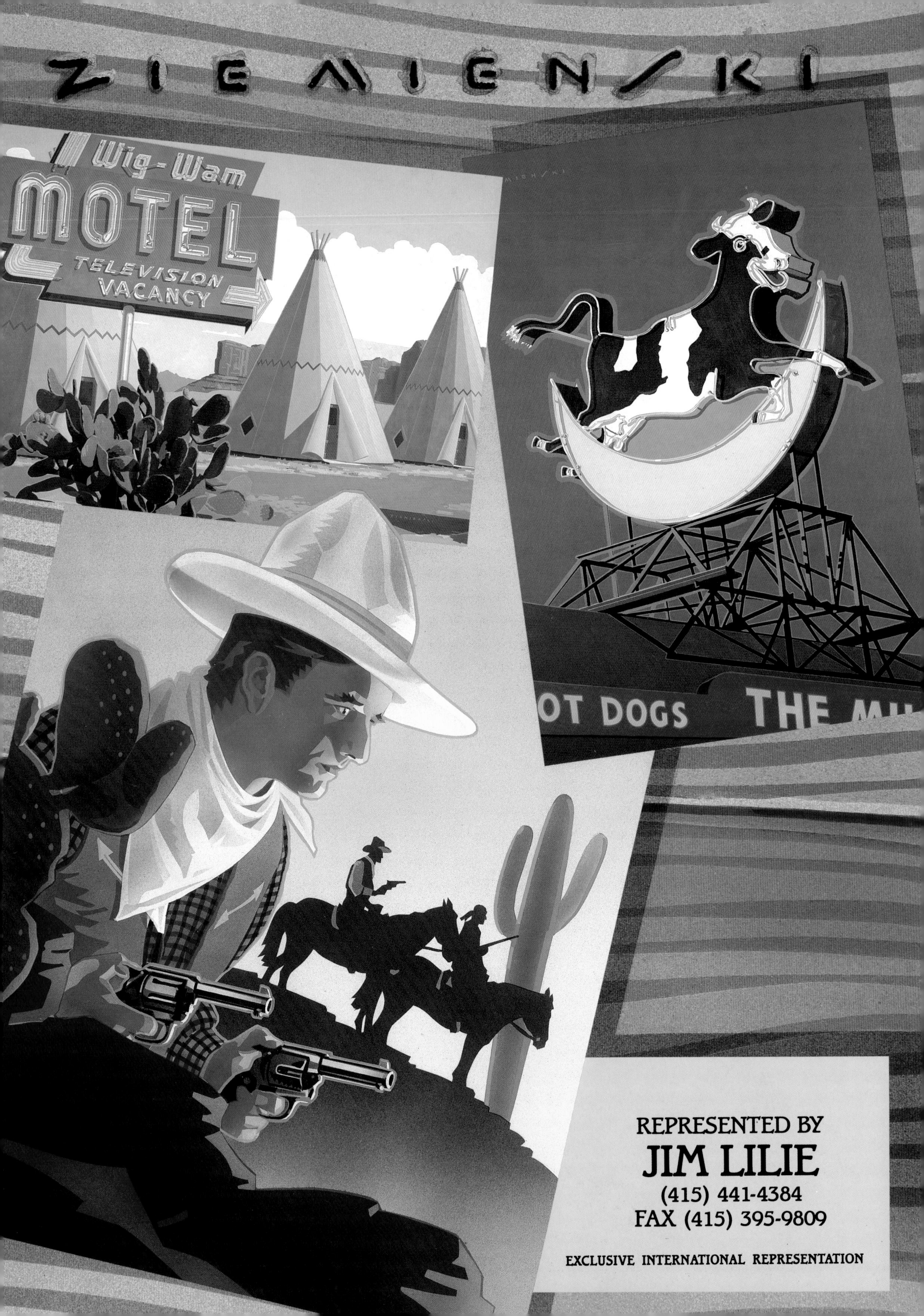
ZIEMIENSKI
Wig-Wam
MOTEL
TELEVISION
VACANCY
REPRESENTED BY
JIM LILIE
(415) 441-4384
FAX (415) 395-9809
EXCLUSIVE INTERNATIONAL REPRESENTATION

DUGALD STERMER [415] 921-8281

Represented by Jim Lilie [415] 441-4384

TVWEEK
SAN FRANCISCO CHRONICLE
SEPTEMBER 10-16, 1989
63RD ANNUAL
Miss America
PAGEANT

RON CHAN

REPRESENTED BY

JIM LILIE

415 441 4384

FAX 415 395 9809

EZRA
EZRA © 1988
Pro Shop
DANGER
EZRA
EZRA
EZRA TUCKER
Illustrator © 1991
Represented by
JIM LILIE
(415) 441-4384

# S T A N   W A T T S

REPRESENTED BY JIM LILIE (415) 441-4384

# CRAIG MARSHALL

*Represented by Jim Lilie (415) 441-4384*

**Hal Lōse**
533 West Hortter Street
Toad Hall
Philadelphia, Pennsylvania 19119
(215) 849-7635
FAX: (215) 849-7635

Member:
Society of Illustrators
Graphic Artists Guild

**John Murray**
(617) 426-0359
FAX: (617) 426-0835

Video available

**Merle Nacht**
374 Main Street
Wethersfield, Connecticut 06109
(203) 563-7993
FAX available

Clients include:
The New Yorker (covers and spot drawings); Conde Nast Traveler; New York; Gourmet; Lotus Magazine; Eltern (W. Germany); The Boston Globe Magazine; The New York Times; Houghton-Mifflin; Harcourt, Brace, Jovanovich; Aetna Insurance; The Travelers Insurance Co.; AAA; United Technologies; Xerox; The Royal Bank; Northeast Utilities; General Electric.

CLIENT: GOURMET

CHICKEN SOUP. CLIENT: APPLAUSE

PRE-THEATER DINNER AD. CLIENT: WATERGATE HOTEL

**Vladimir M. Pechanec**
34-43 Crescent Street
Long Island City
New York, New York 11106
(718) 729-3973

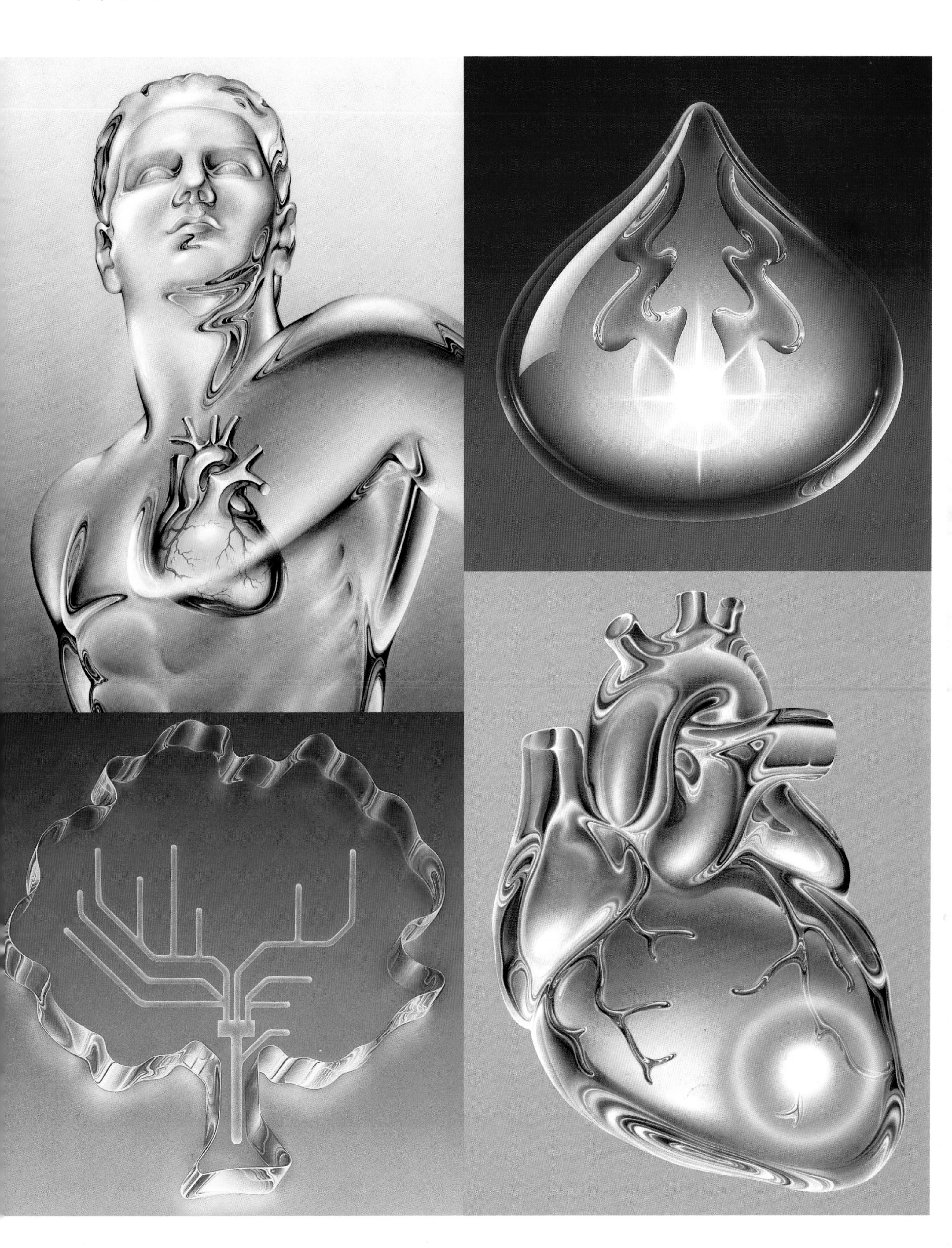

**ED RENFRO** 250 E. 83D STREET, APT. 4E, NEW YORK, N.Y. 10028, (212) 879-3823

**Bot Roda**
78 Victoria Lane
Lancaster, Pennsylvania 17603
(717) 393-1406
FAX: (717) 299-5861

Humorous Illustration for Editorial, Advertising and Corporate usage.

Amtrak, AT&T, Cowles Magazines, Cracked Magazine, Field & Stream, Kellogg's, Lintas: NY, National Lampoon, Outdoor Life, R.R.Donnelly & Sons, Skiing, Wyeth-Aherst Labs, Young & Rubicam.

Finalist Humor '88, Member Society of Illustrators

Work can also be seen in Humor 2 and RSVP 15.

**Jeffrey Seaver**
130 West 24th Street, #4B
New York, New York 10011-1906
(212) 741-2279
FAX: (212) 255-3823

**Kurt Shaw**
2954 Sheraden Boulevard
Pittsburgh, Pennsylvania 15204
(412) 771-7345
FAX in studio

Clients Include:
The Ad Report
Complete Woman
Cosmopolitan
Gannett
King Features Syndicate
McDonald's Corporation
Pittsburgh Magazine
PNC Financial Corporation
The Rotarian
The Saturday Evening Post
Westinghouse Electric Corporation
Woman
Woman's World

PITTSBURGH'S BUSINESS MAGAZINE

EXECUTIVE REPORT

January 19

Who Promotes Pittsburgh?

SPECIAL REPORT
Commercial Real Estate

Economic Development Profile: Northern West Virginia

**John Sposato**
43 East 22nd Street
New York, New York 10010
(212) 477-3909

Illustration, Design, Lettering
In Oil Pastel

Clients:
Federal Express, Pepsi, Coca-Cola, Sony, Gulf + Western, Timex, Nabisco, Marriott Hotels, Hyatt Hotels, Estée Lauder, Winston-Salem, Playboy, The Atlantic, Esquire, Newsweek, New York Magazine, Massachusetts Lottery, Paramount Pictures, HBO, NBC, CBS Records, Random House, Simon & Schuster, Warner Books.

Awards:
Society of Illustrators, Art Directors Club Annual, Graphis Annual, Graphis Posters, American Institute of Graphic Arts, CA Annual, CA Art Annual, Andy Awards.

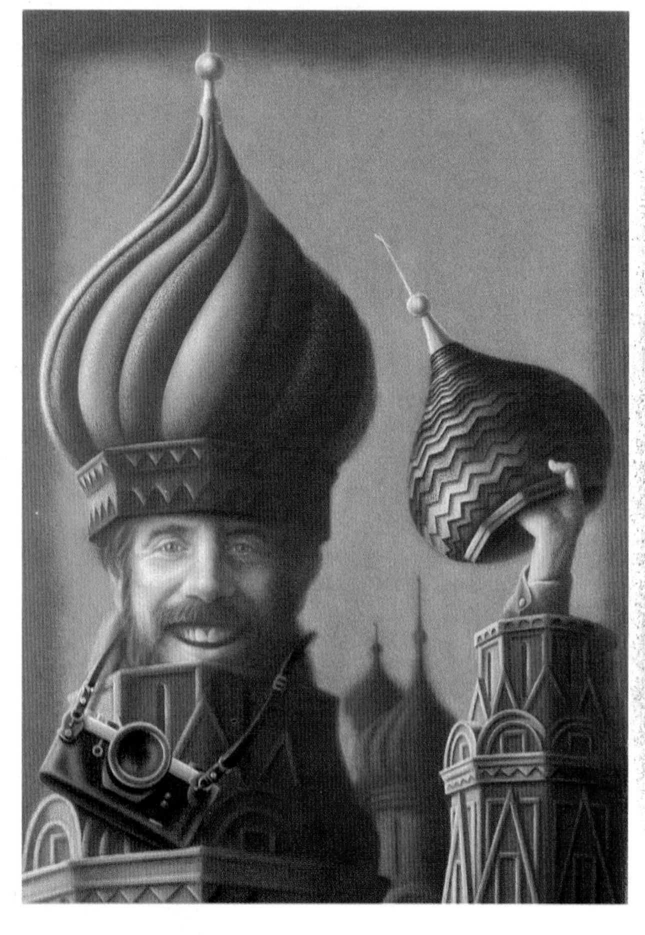

**John Sposato**
43 East 22nd Street
New York, New York 10010
(212) 477-3909

Illustration, Design, Lettering
In Oil Pastel

Clients:
Federal Express, Pepsi, Coca-Cola, Sony, Gulf + Western, Timex, Nabisco, Marriott Hotels, Hyatt Hotels, Estée Lauder, Winston-Salem, Playboy, The Atlantic, Esquire, Newsweek, New York Magazine, Massachusetts Lottery, Paramount Pictures, HBO, NBC, CBS Records, Random House, Simon & Schuster, Warner Books.

Awards:
Society of Illustrators, Art Directors Club Annual, Graphis Annual, Graphis Posters, American Institute of Graphic Arts, CA Annual, CA Art Annual, Andy Awards.

Above clockwise: Federal Express, Marriott Hotels, Bermuda Tourism

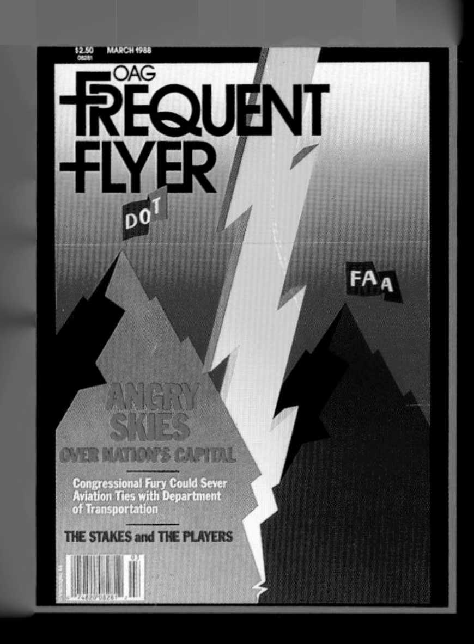

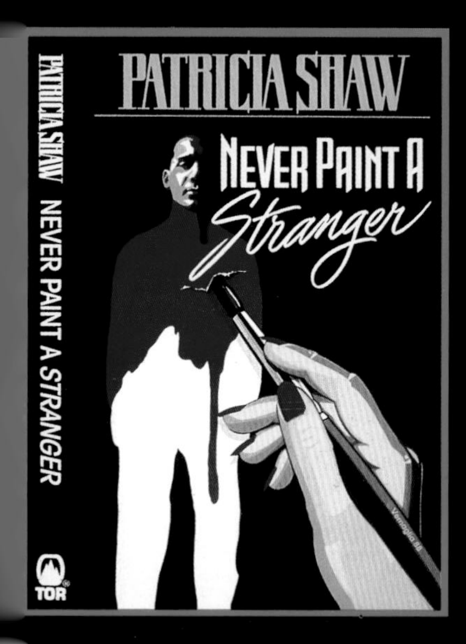


Top: Cover Design, Frequent Flyer Magazine, March, 1988. **Above**: Tor Books, Publishers, Cover Design, 1989.

Commissioned "**Official**" **Logo of the Birthplace of Baseball** adopted by the State of New Jersey on June 19th, 1990. Presented to President Bush, Vice President Quayle and every member of the US Senate and Congress. Pending congressional approval as national symbol of Baseball Day.

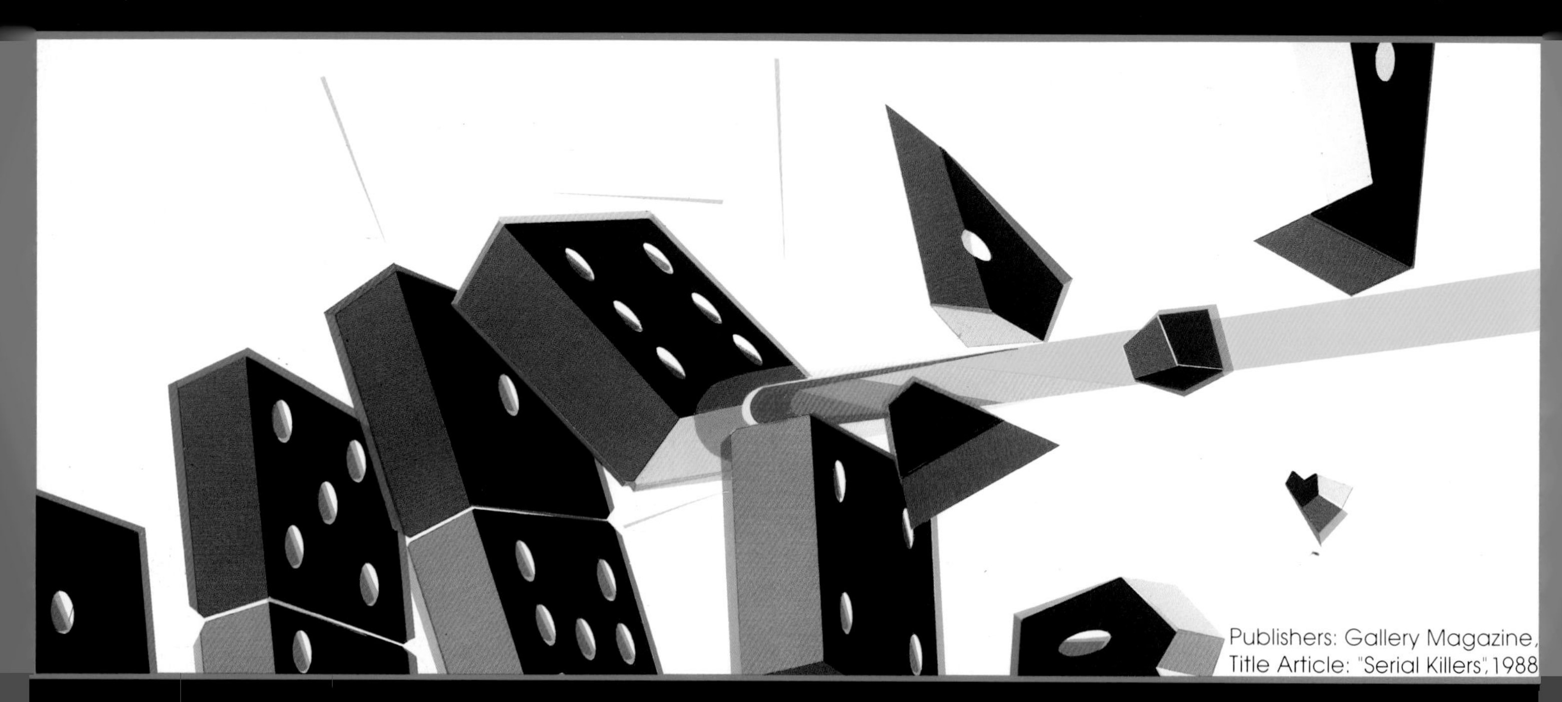

Publishers: Gallery Magazine, Title Article: "Serial Killers",1988

# VERNAGLIA

REPRESENTED BY:
CHUCK DeMARCO
OFFICE/FAX: 201-865-4483

Promotion: Corporate Daycare

Michael Vernaglia Artworks, Inc. • Studio: 201-792-4894 • FAX: 201-659-7750

**Terry Sirrell**
768 Red Oak Drive
Bartlett, Illinois 60103
(708) 213-9003
FAX in Studio

Partial Client List:
Leo Burnett Adv.; Ted Bates Adv.; J. Walter Thompson Adv.; Dawson Johns & Black Adv.; Bozell, Jacobs, Kenyon & Eckhardt Adv.; Frankel & Co.; BBDO Adv.; Campbell Mithun Esty Adv.; D.D.B. Needham Adv.; Bayer Bess Vanderwarker Advertising; Garfield-Linn & Company Advertising. Anheuser-Busch; Ralston Purina Co.; Chicago Cubs; Cracker Jack; National Safety Council; McDonald's; Scholastic Pub.; Unocal 76; Cap'n Crunch Cereal; Quaker Oats Co.; Kellogg's; Hinckley & Schmitt; Woman's World Magazine; Woman's Day Magazine; Barron's; Harcourt Brace Jovanovich; Humor '87.

# Illustrators

## Canada
## Canada
## Kanada

# BEHA

TÉL: (514) 843-3219•5193 RUE CARTIER MONTRÉAL, QUÉBEC H2H 1X6•FAX: (514) 843-3219

# NINA BERKSON

400 Dowd Montreal Canada H2Z 1B7
(514) 878 2359 • 286 2970

CLAF

CLAUDE LAFRANCE
(514) 255 3919

VICKY ELSOM 3-D PRODUCTIONS 95 LAWTON BLVD., TORONTO, ONTARIO M4V 1Z8 (416) 489-6453

PHOTOGRAPHY — CLOCKWISE from top, RAY BOUDREAU, STEVE LIVINGSTON, RAY BOUDREAU

# Rob MacDougall

4 1 6 • 8 4 7 • 7 6 6 3

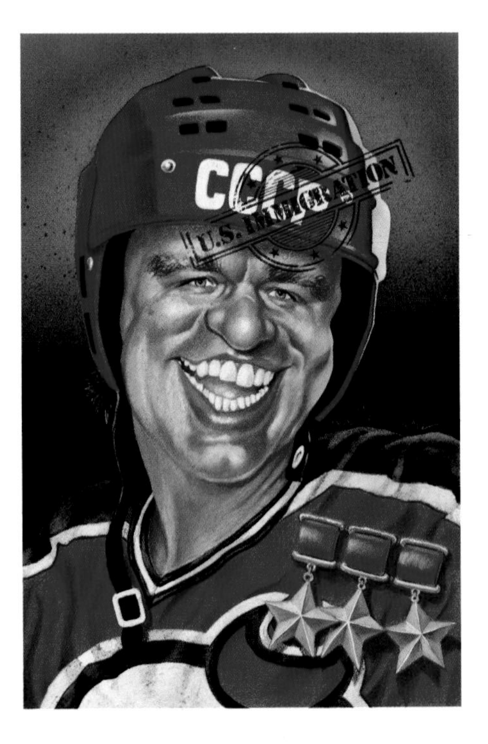

# A L A I N   M A S S I C O T T E

(514) 843-4169

1121, rue
Ste-Catherine
ouest
4e étage
Montréal,
Québec
H3B 1J5

Tél.:(514)
843- 4169
Fax:(514)
849-5955
ACPIP/
CAPIC
AIIQ

PAUL MORIN, R.R. 4 ROCKWOOD, ONTARIO, CANADA NOB 2K0 (519) 833-9906, FAX IN STUDIO, 40 MINUTES WEST OF TORONTO

▲ KILIMANJARO ELEPHANT PROJECT ■ THE ORPHAN BOY, OXFORD UNIVERSITY PRESS ● ASSANTI SANA, LIMITED EDITION PRINT

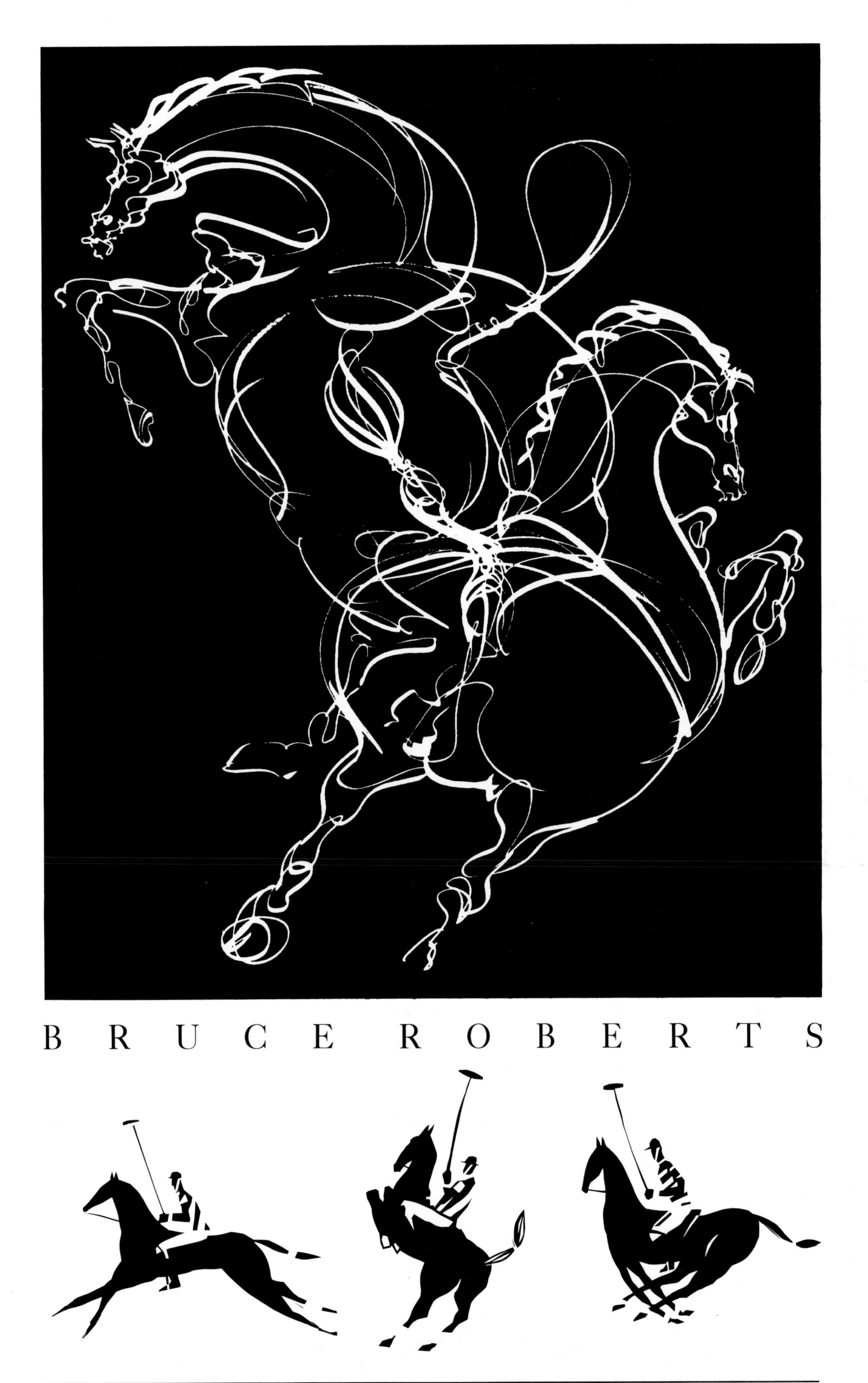
B R U C E R O B E R T S
60 de Bresoles #205 MONTRÉAL, Canada H2Y 1V5 (514) 849-1001

Luc Normandin
5031 rue Sherbrooke O., suite 9
Montréal, Québec H4A 1S8
(514) 489-1172
AIIQ — ACPIP

◀ Magazine L'Actualité
D.A.: Danielle Le Bel

▼ La Maison de la Création
D.A.: France Le Bon

# BRUCE ROBERTS 514·849·1001

ONE A.M.

Affie Mohammed
33 Wasdale Crescent Apt 9
Toronto Ontario M6A 1W9
416 • 782-5113

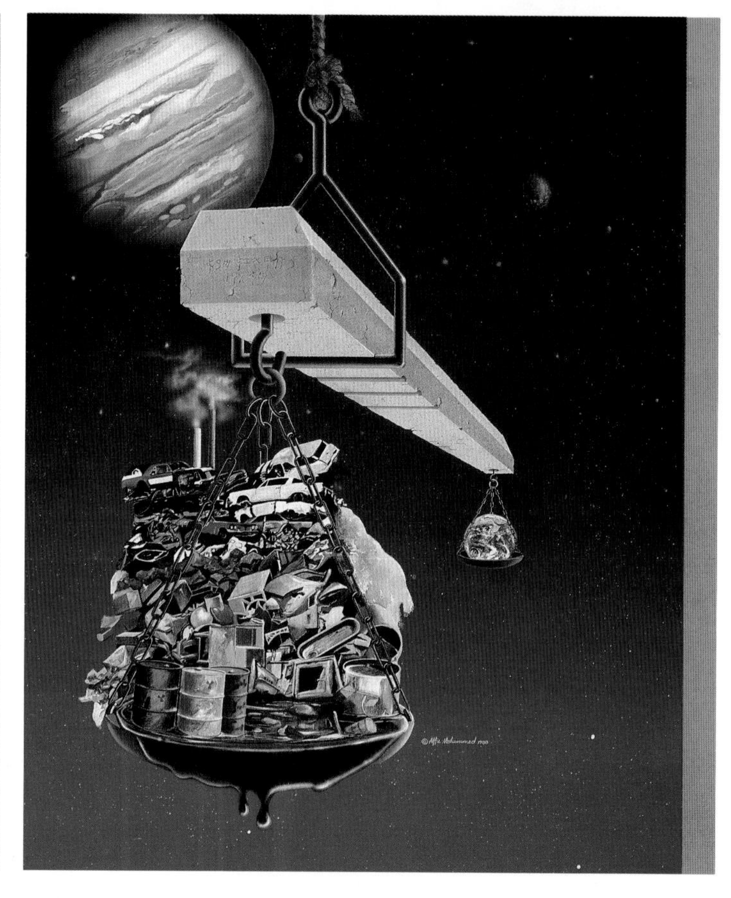

# MARION STUCK

416·567·1493

# Robert Johannsen

416 · 567 · 1493

JOHN TATE • 164 POPLAR DRIVE, DOLLARD DES ORMEAUX, MTL., Qc. H9A 2A7 • 514-684-1906

**Gordon Weber**
**Illustrations**

6 Nanook Crescent
Kanata Ontario
Canada K2L 2A7
(613) 592-8826

CAPIC

# Illustrators

## Chile
## Chili
## Chile

# LINCOLN FUENTES

Hamburgo 365-Y
Ñuñoa
Santiago
Chile
Tel. 227 11 90

Airbrush illustration for major advertising agencies, such as: J. Walter Thompson, Lintas-Chile, Azocar, Morrison & Walker, Northcote & Asociados Ogilvy & Mather, McCann-Erickson, Epoca Ted Bates.

Realiza ilustraciones en aerógrafo para las principales agencias de publicidad tales como: J. Walter Thompson, Lintas-Chile, Azocar, Morrison & Walker, Northcote & Asociados Ogilvy & Mather, McCann-Erickson, Epoca Ted Bates.

Illustrations à l'aérographe pour les plus grandes agences de publicité, telles que: J. Walter Thompson, Lintas-Chile, Azocar, Morrison & Walker, Northcote & Asociados Ogilvy & Mather, McCann-Erickson, Epoca Ted Bates.

# Illustrators

## Hong Kong
## Hongkong
## Hong Kong

CHEONG, LUK WAI 94-95
CHEUNG CHI KWONG, ERIC 99
LENEVEU, HELENE 98
MEKISIC, ZORAN 96-97

# LUK WAI CHEONG

3306 Ka Wing House
Ka Tin Court
N. T.
Hong Kong
Tel. 697 65 45
Fax. +852-602 09 83

Illustrator

Illustrateur

Illustrator

# LUK WAI CHEONG

3306 Ka Wing House
Ka Tin Court
N. T.
Hong Kong
Tel. 697 65 45
Fax. +852-602 09 83

Illustrator

Illustrateur

Illustrator

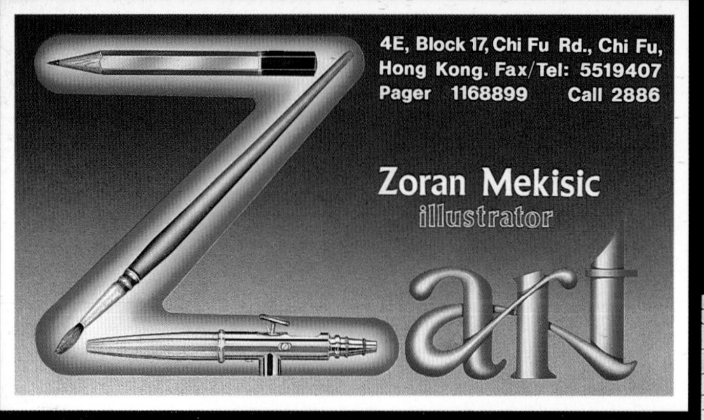

4E, Block 17, Chi Fu Rd., Chi Fu,
Hong Kong. Fax/Tel: 5519407
Pager 1168899 Call 2886
Zoran Mekisic
illustrator
Zart


# Zoran Mekisic
## illustrator
## 5519407

Cover for 'Far Eastern Economic Review'

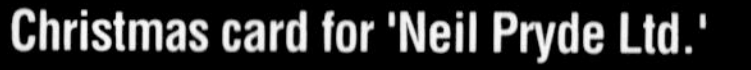

Christmas card for 'Neil Pryde Ltd.'

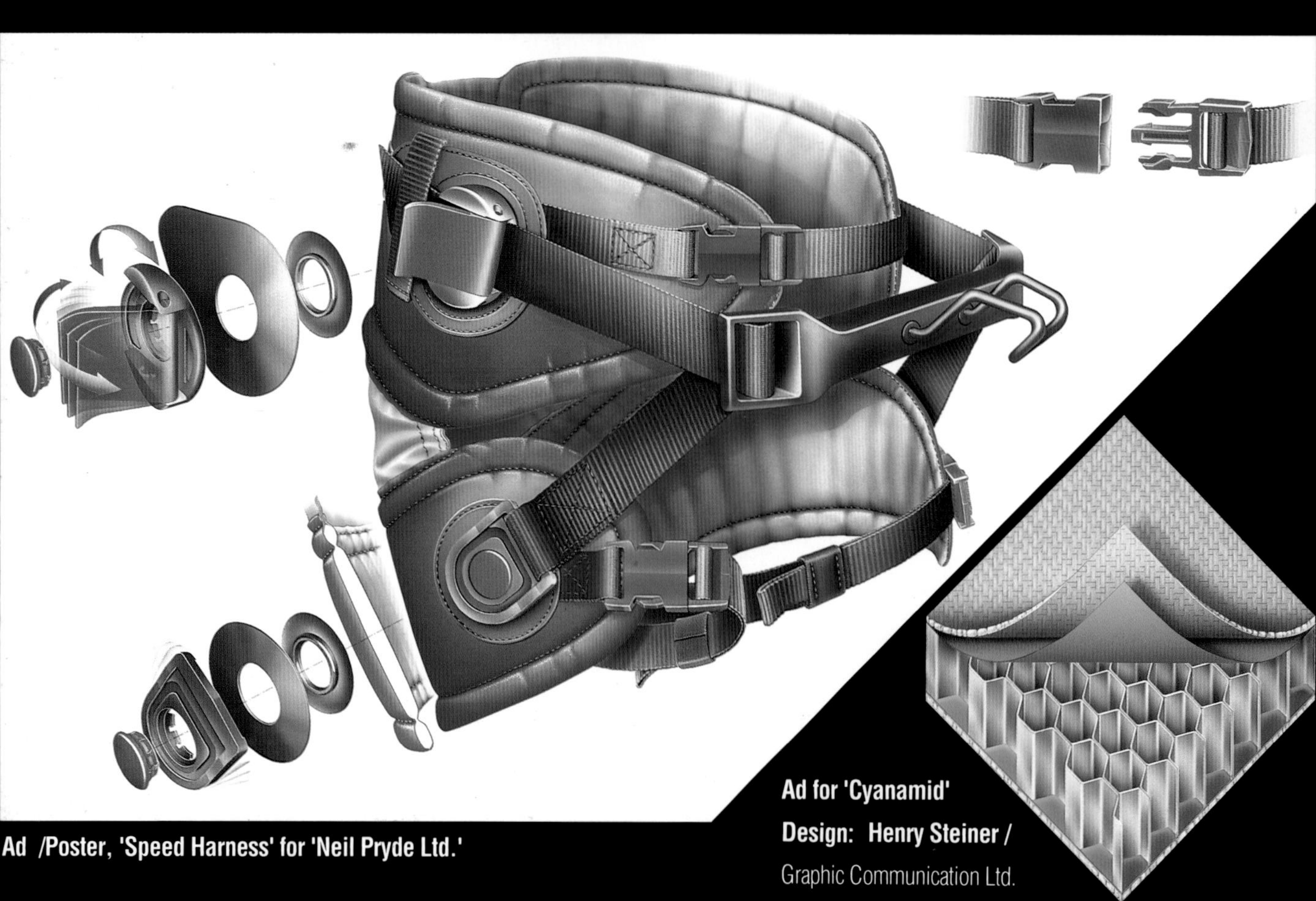

Ad /Poster, 'Speed Harness' for 'Neil Pryde Ltd.'

Ad for 'Cyanamid'

Design: Henry Steiner /

Graphic Communication Ltd.

Cover for 'Asia Magazine'

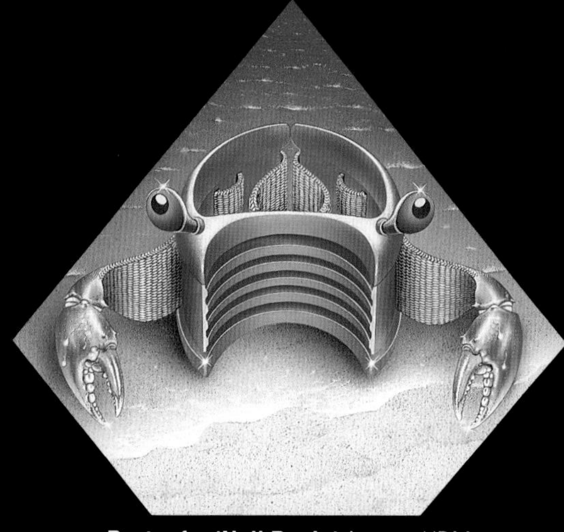

**Poster for 'Neil Pryde'** Agency: HDM

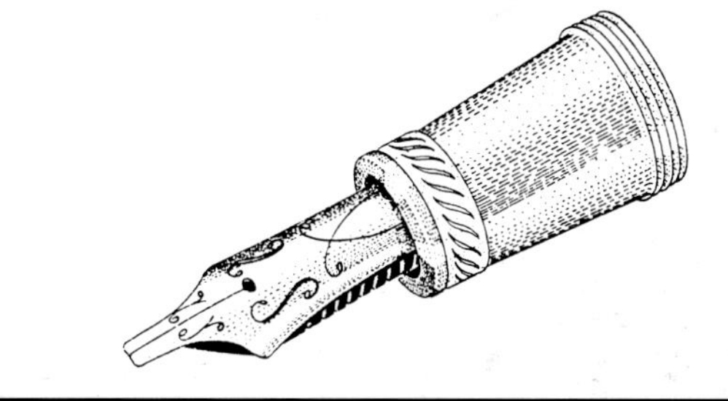

**Covers, 'The Peninsula Group'** Agency: Saatchi and Saatchi

Cover for 'Asia Magazine'

Self Promotion

**HELENE LENEVEU**

92 Robinson Road, 6/F
Mid Levels
Hong Kong
Tel. 858 85 29

THE ECCENTRIC

TIME TO GET OFF THE BOOZE, MARCEL

THE DISHES SYMPHONY

PIGS

SERENADE

FARANDOLE

TALKING TO THE MOON

**ERIC CHEUNG CHI KWONG**
No. A2 7/F Paramount Mansion
389 Chatham Road North
Kowloon
Hong Kong
Tel. 364 18 36
Pager: 1168923 A/C 8229

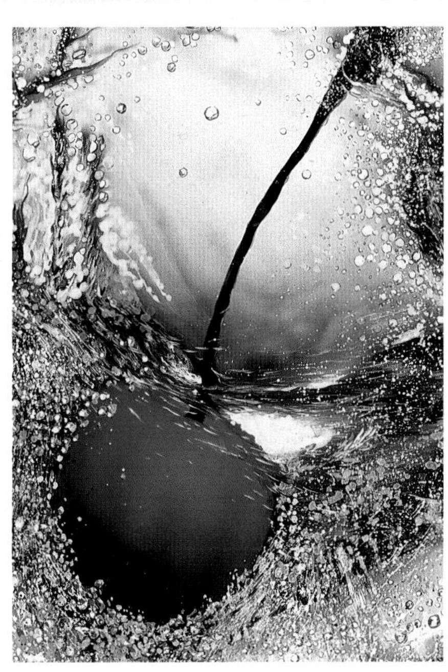

# Illustrators

## Japan
## Japon
## Japan

# MARIKO ABE

STAFF ILLUSTRATION JIGYOBU

Shinwa Building
2-9-2 Nishitenma
Kita-ku
Osaka 530
Japan
Tel. 06-363 4963
Fax: 06-363 4937

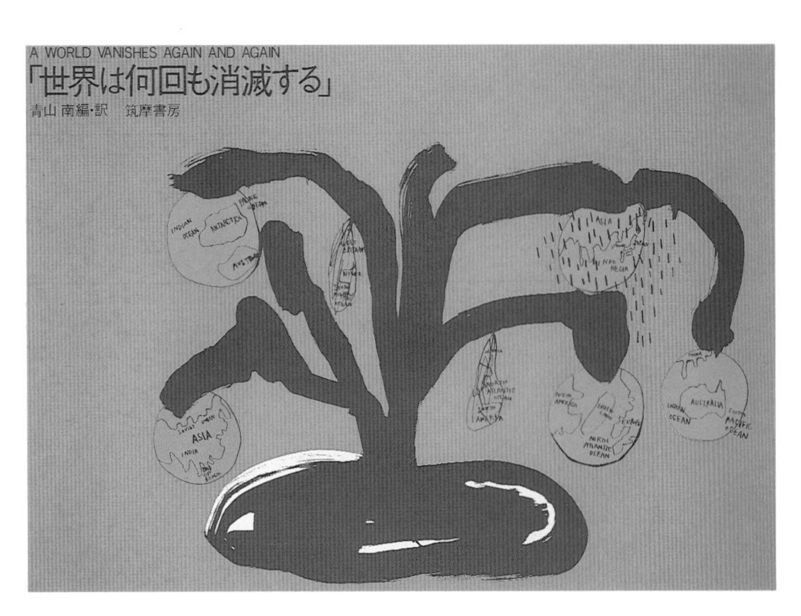

A WORLD VANISHES AGAIN AND AGAIN
「世界は何回も消滅する」
青山 南編・訳　筑摩書房

# MARIKO ABE

STAFF ILLUSTRATION JIGYOBU

Shinwa Building
2-9-2 Nishitenma
Kita-ku
Osaka 530
Japan
Tel. 06-363 4963
Fax: 06-363 4937


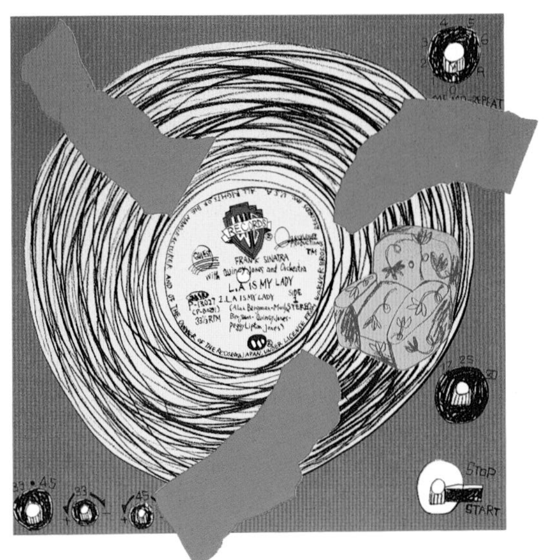

# MASATO ARAI

8-9-6 Shakujii-cho
Nerima-ku
Tokyo 177
Japan
Tel. 03-3996 0676
Fax: 03-3996 0676

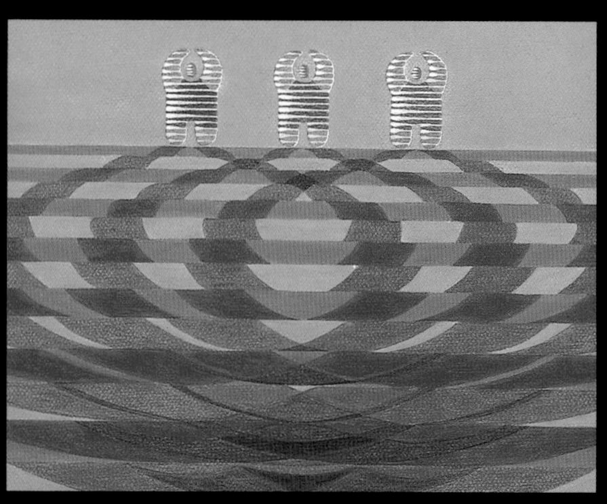

## TADAO FURUTA

503 Denken Kyodo Dai-1 Mansion
5-33-3 Kyodo
Setagaya-ku
Tokyo 156
Japan
Tel. 03-3426 2819

# SHUHEI EGUCHI

5-B Kyoritsukosan Shiroganedai Bldg.
5-3-3 Shiroganedai
Minato-ku
Tokyo 108
Japan
Tel. 03-3473 8423

**SHUHEI EGUCHI**

5-B Kyoritsukosan Shiroganedai Bldg.
5-3-3 Shiroganedai
Minato-ku
Tokyo 108
Japan
Tel. 03-3473 8423

## CHARLOTTE FUJIKAKE

702 Ars Nakameguro
1-3-3 Higashiyama
Meguro-ku
Tokyo 153
Japan
Tel. 03-3719 1244

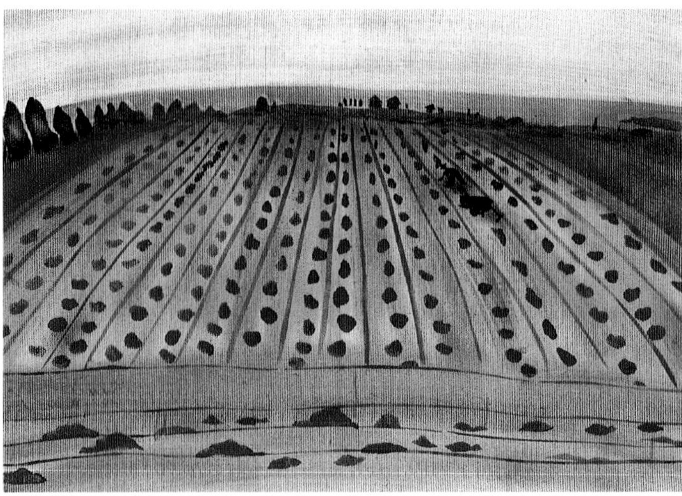

# MASAKUNI FUJIKAKE

702 Ars Nakameguro
1-3-3 Higashiyama
Meguro-ku
Tokyo 153
Japan
Tel. 03-3719 1244

# HIROYUKI FUJIWARA

301 Corpo Nemu
2-11-3 Takada No Baba
Shinjuku-ku
Tokyo 169
Japan
Tel. 03-3232 0843
Fax: 03-3208 2449

▲ Paradise Alley: I (Asakusa, Tokyo)
Japanese Restaurant "Yoshino-ya„
1041 × 762 mm (Silk-screen)

# HIROYUKI FUJIWARA

301 Corpo Nemu
2-11-3 Takada No Baba
Shinjuku-ku
Tokyo 169
Japan
Tel. 03-3232 0843
Fax: 03-3208 2449

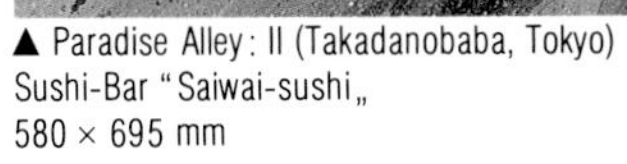
▲ Paradise Alley: II (Takadanobaba, Tokyo)
Sushi-Bar "Saiwai-sushi„
580 × 695 mm

▲ Paradise Alley: III (Tsukishima, Tokyo)
"Tsukishima Kan'non„ 285 × 427 mm

▼ Japanese Candys 450 × 210 mm

# KAZUO HAKAMADA

6-13-15-406 Toyotama Kita
Nerima-ku
Tokyo 176
Japan
Tel. 03-5999 2383
Fax: 03-5999 2383

Agent:
POINT DELTA & ATY GROUP, INC.
Yasuhisa Azuma
295 Madison Ave., Suite # 926
New York, NY 10017
Tel. 212-949 7639
Fax: 212-949 7633

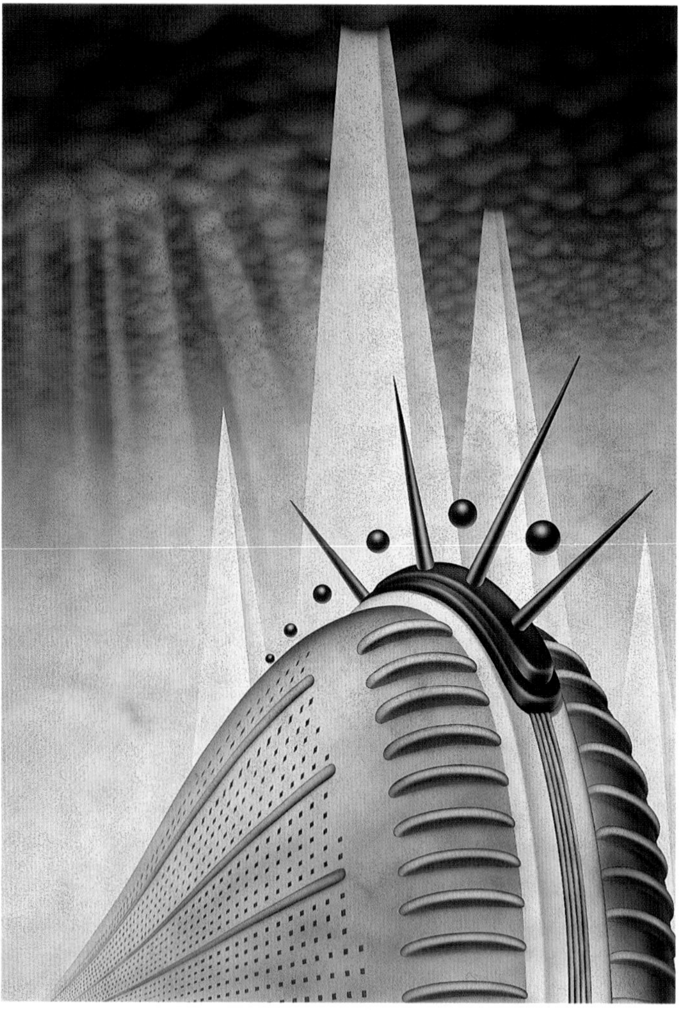

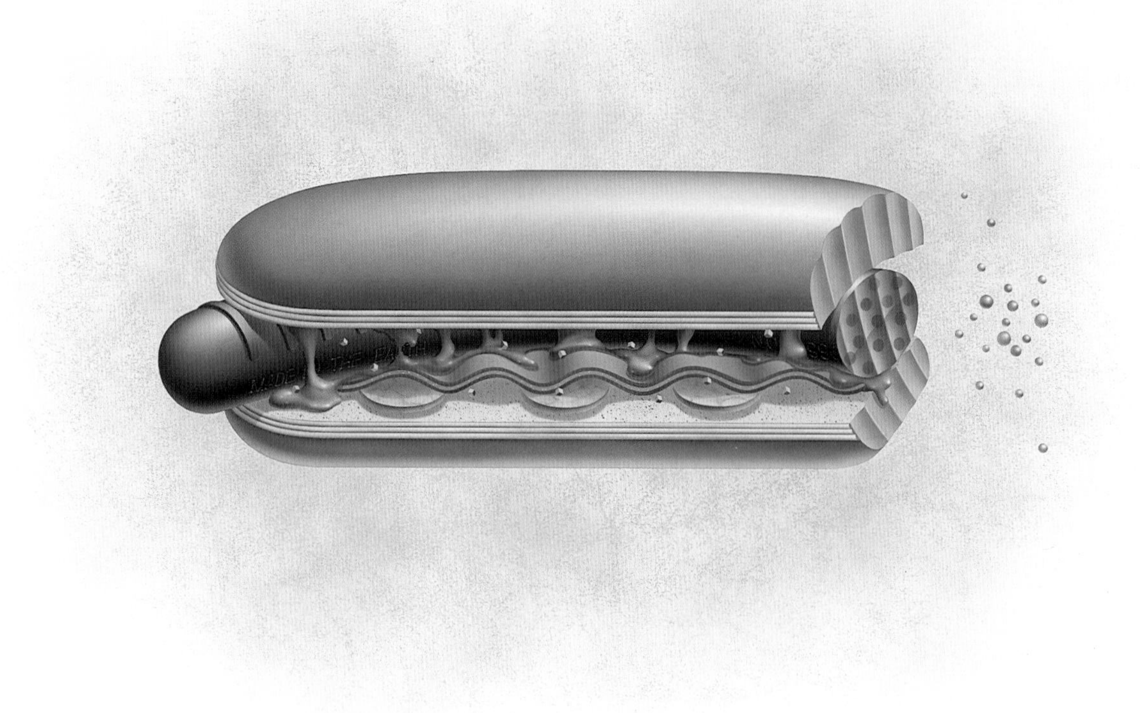

# KEIKO HIRANO

301 An House Kaminoge
1-25-13 Kaminoge
Setagaya-ku
Tokyo 158
Japan
Tel. 03-5706 6548

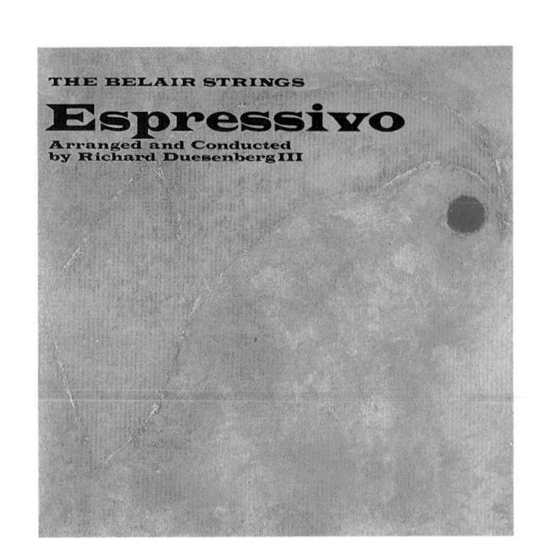

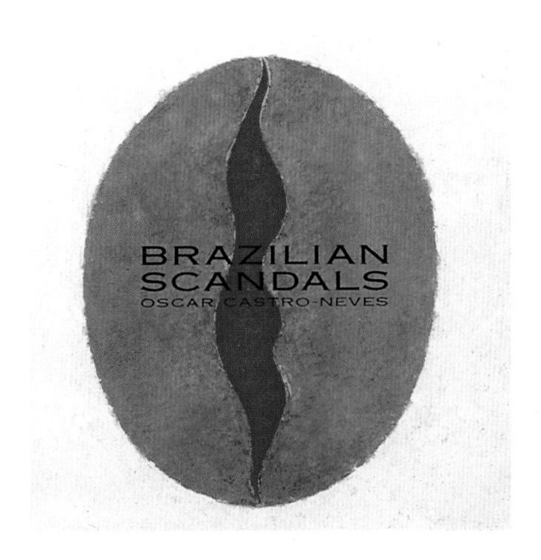


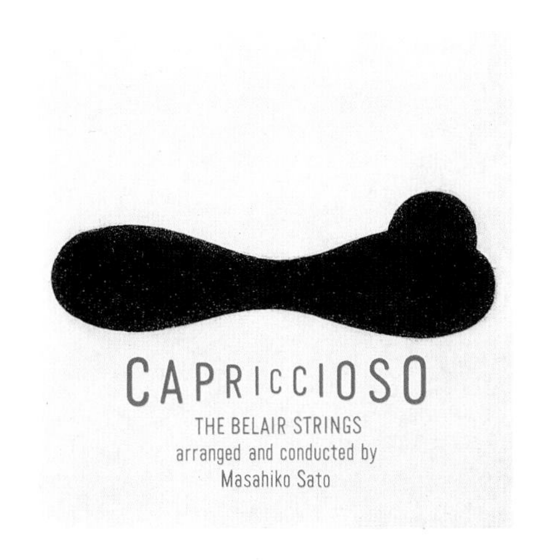

# HIDEO IGAWA

3-A Arubosu
5-31-17 Okusawa
Setagaya-ku
Tokyo 158
Japan
Tel. 03-3722 6479

## SHUN ITAGAKI

5-16-10-402 Minami Azabu
Minato-ku
Tokyo 106
Japan
Tel. 03-3446 8300

# KENICHI KANNO

203 Yoyogi Panbial Bldg.
1-2-4 Tomigaya
Shibuya-ku
Tokyo 151
Japan
Tel. 03-3467 9484

# HISAO KAWADA

1001 Nisho Iwai Honancho Mansion
1-51-7 Honan
Suginami-ku
Tokyo 168
Japan
Tel. 03-3328 8906

## OSAMU KAWAMURA

302 Harajuku Jitorunku
4-15-16 Jingumae
Shibuya-ku
Tokyo 150
Japan
Tel. 03-3403 3343

# HIDEYUKI KAWARASAKI

5-6-6-403 Tsurukawa
Machida City
Tokyo 194-01
Japan
Tel. 0427-34 4677

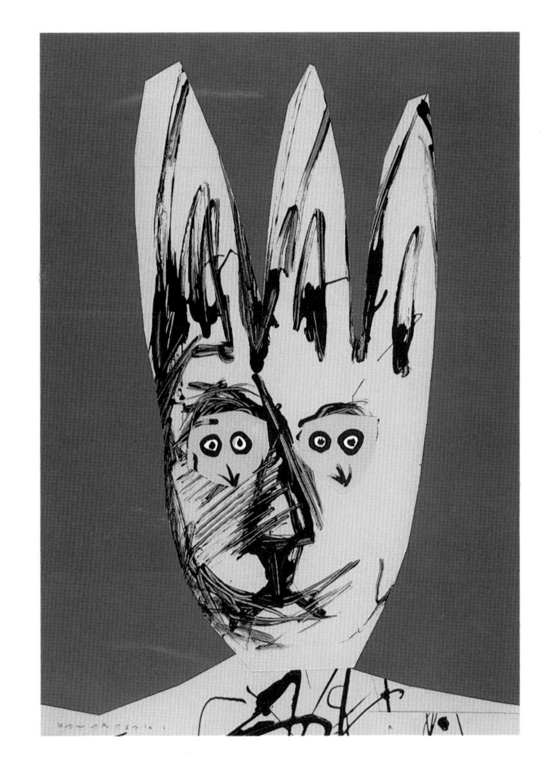

# SADAHITO MORI

55-3 Wakakusa-cho
Minami-ku
Nagoya City
Aichi 457
Japan
Tel. 052-823 2909

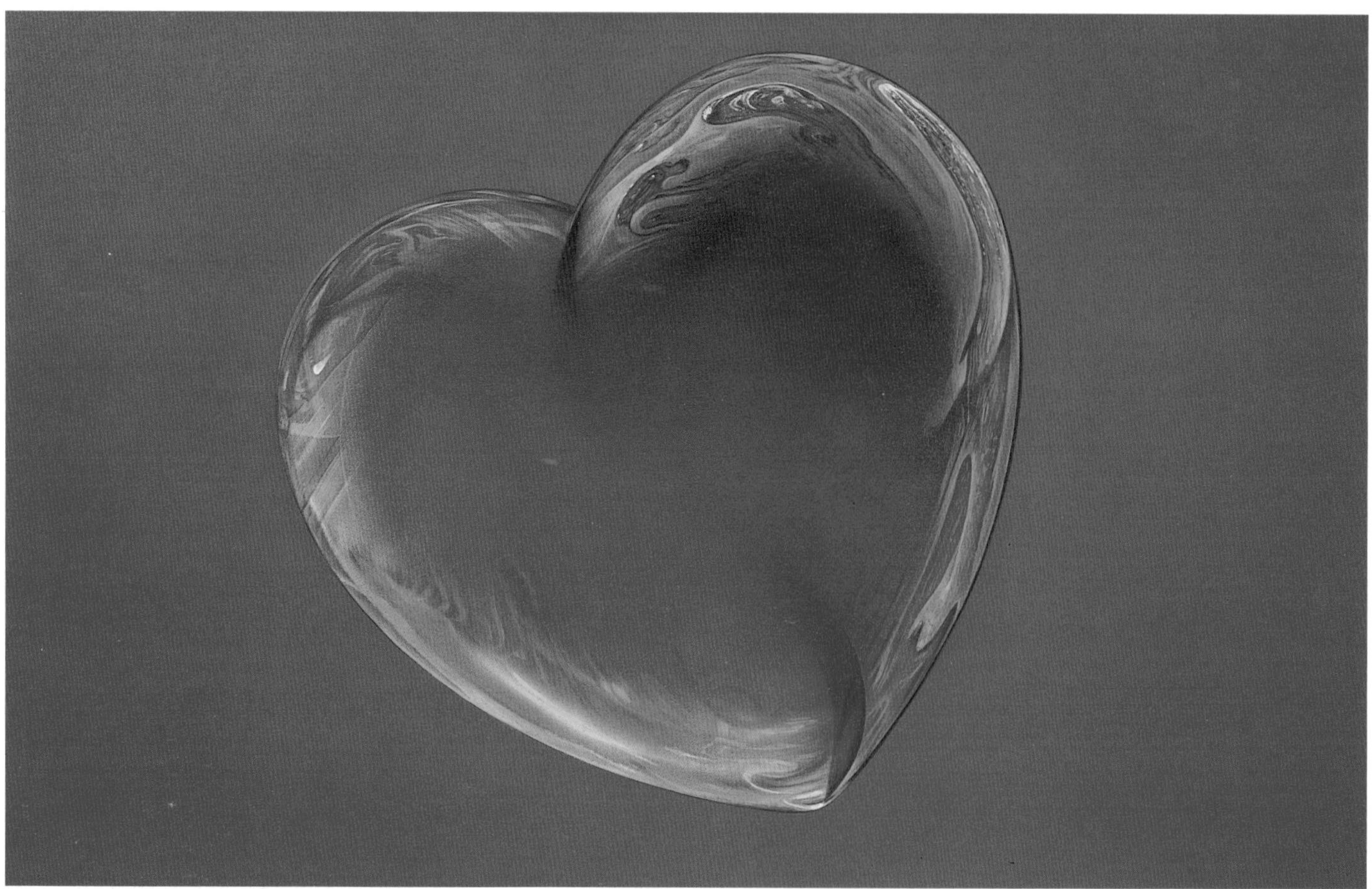

## SADAHITO MORI

55-3 Wakakusa-cho
Minami-ku
Nagoya City
Aichi 457
Japan
Tel. 052-823 2909

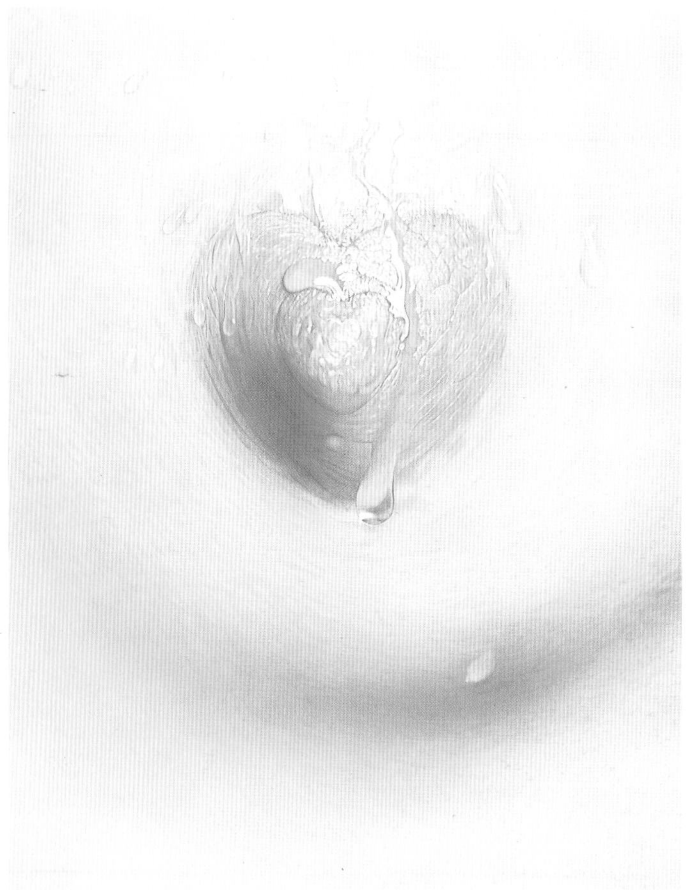

# TAKAHIRO NAGINO

401 Le Soleil
2-3-4 Sendagaya
Shibuya-ku
Tokyo 151
Japan
Tel. 03-3479 6975
Fax: 03-3408 2478

# HIDE NAKAJIMA

STAFF, INC.
410-8 Kameino
Fujisawa-City
Kanagawa 252
Japan
Tel. 0466-82-9638
Fax: 0466-82-9638

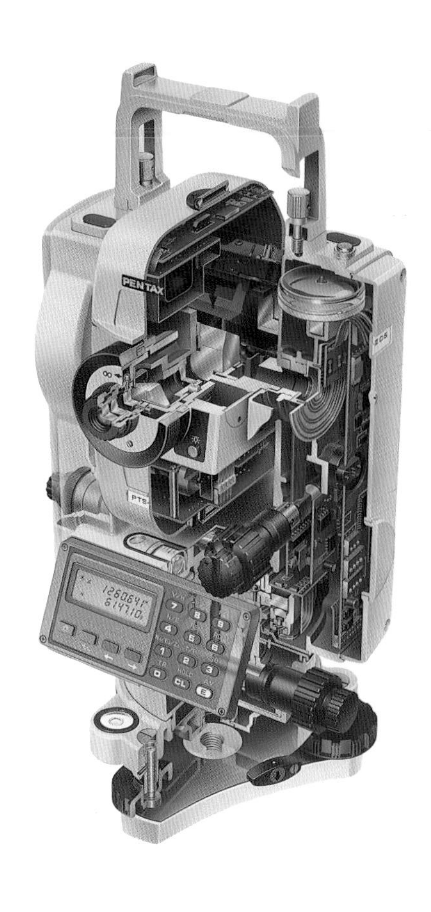

# KAZUMI OGAWA

101 Arusu Zama Tatsunodai
75-1 Tatsunodai
Zama City
Kanagawa 228
Japan
Tel. 0462-57 2477
Fax: 0462-57 2478

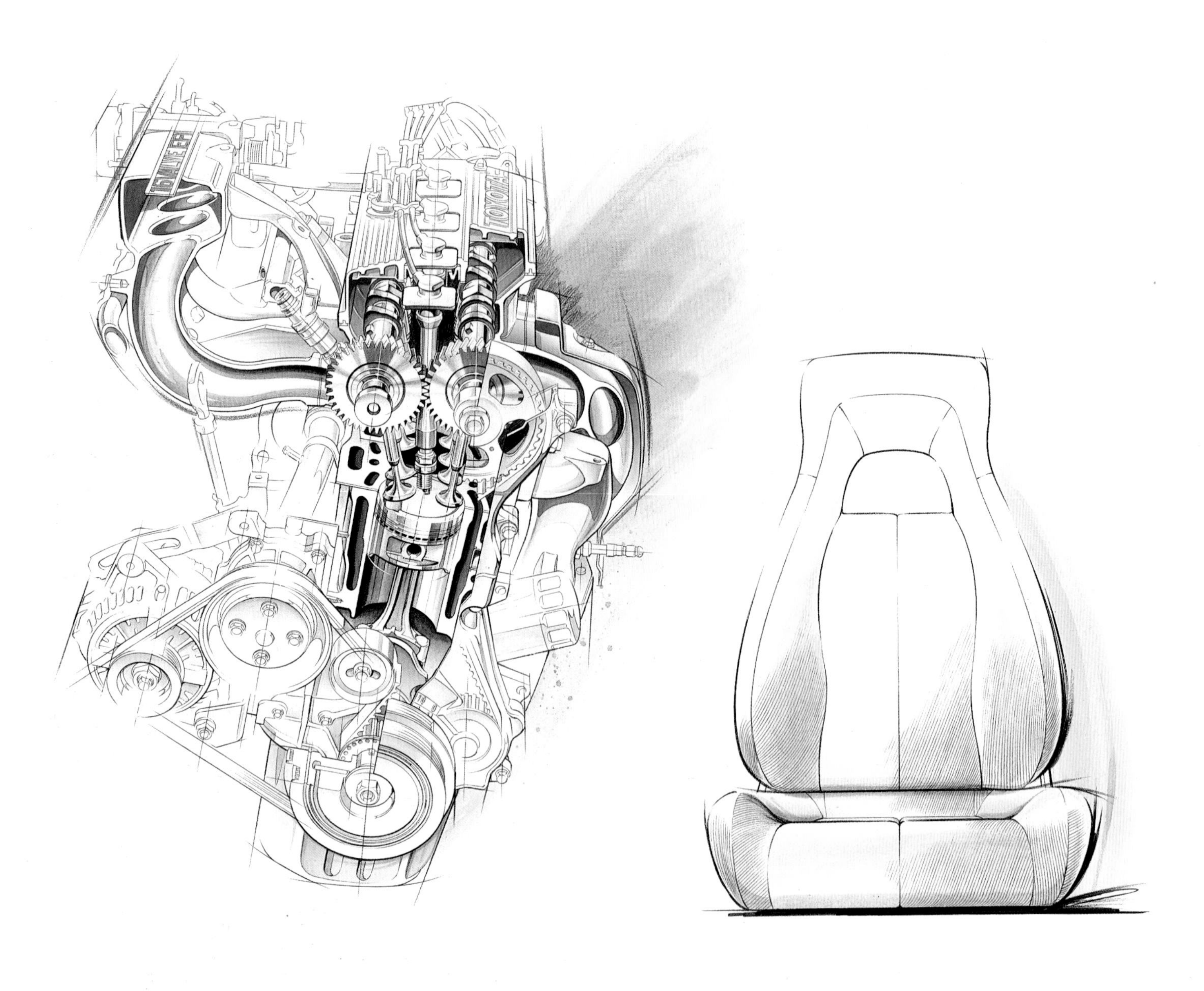

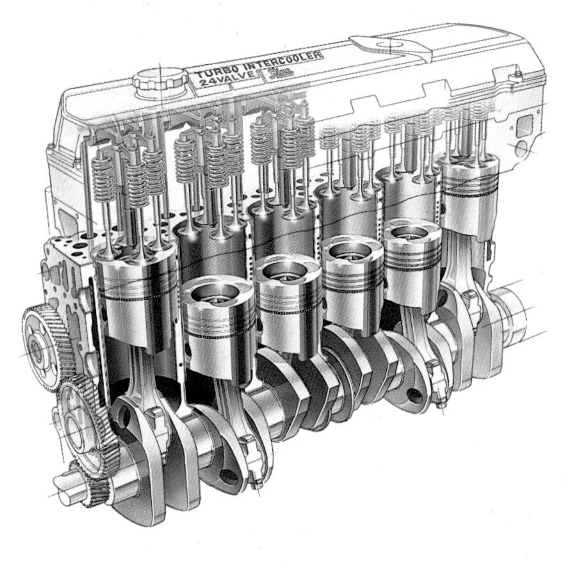


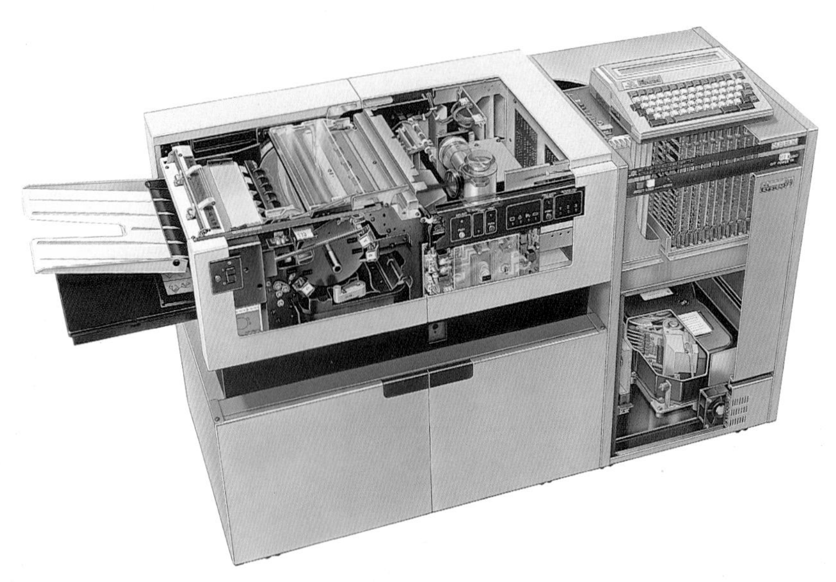

## TAKAAKI OKUDA

203 Berubyu Musashino
3-10-13 Nishiogi Kita
Suginami-ku
Tokyo 167
Japan
Tel. 03-3301 9659

**HARECHIKA SAKAI**

986-6 Ooeda
Kasukabe City
Saitama 344
Japan
Tel. 048-736 9845

## HARECHIKA SAKAI

986-6 Ooeda
Kasukabe City
Saitama 344
Japan
Tel. 048-736 9845

## TOYOHIKO SATO

STUDIO SUPER, INC.

1-43-23-303 Tomigaya
Shibuya-ku
Tokyo 151
Japan
Tel. 03-3468 1657

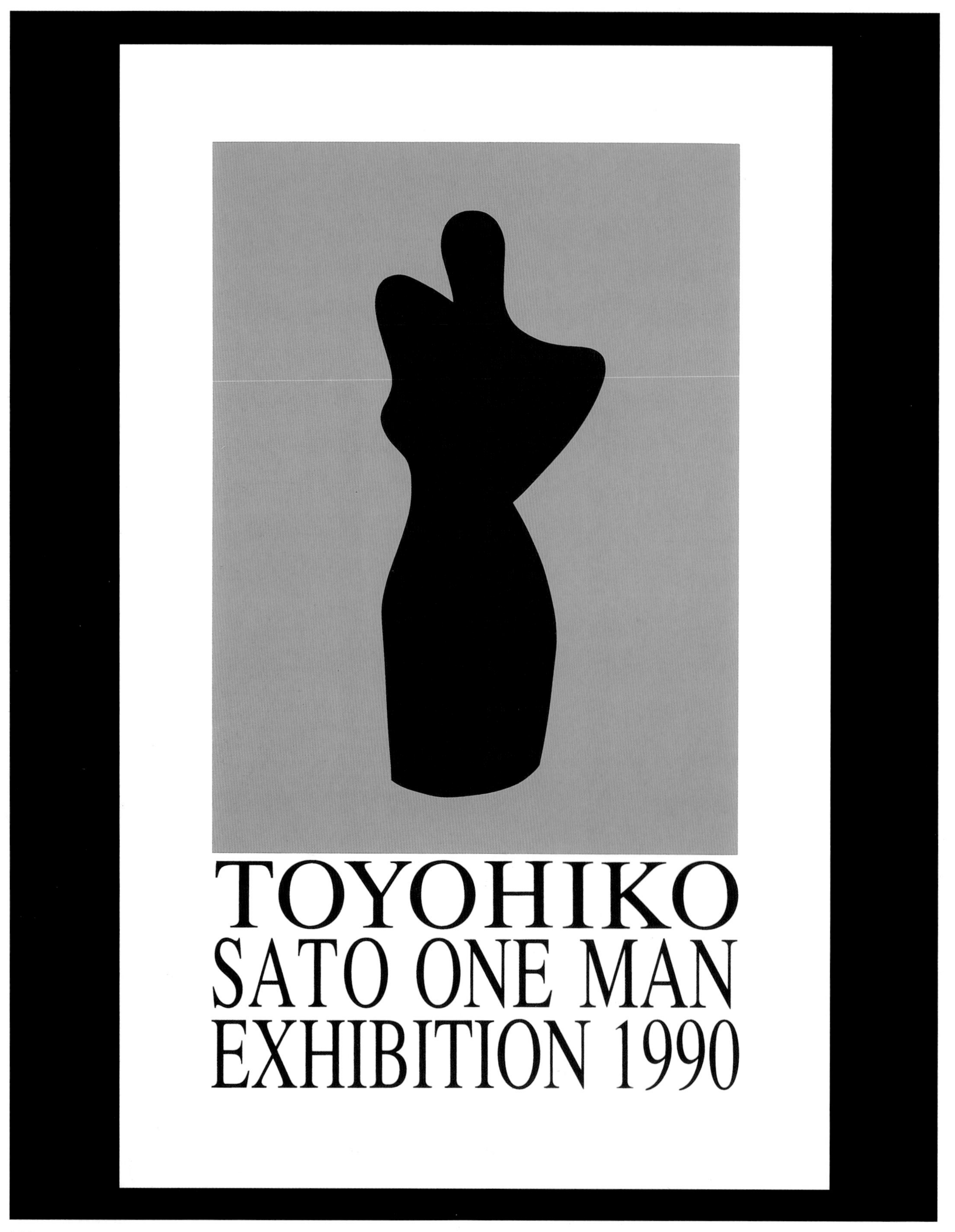

# TOYOHIKO SATO

STUDIO SUPER, INC.

1-43-23-303 Tomigaya
Shibuya-ku
Tokyo 151
Japan
Tel. 03-3468 1657

# TATSUMI SEKINE


206 Green Park Kawasaki
3-1-3 Fujisaki
Kawasaki-ku
Kawasaki City
Kanagawa 210
Japan
Tel. 044-266 6110


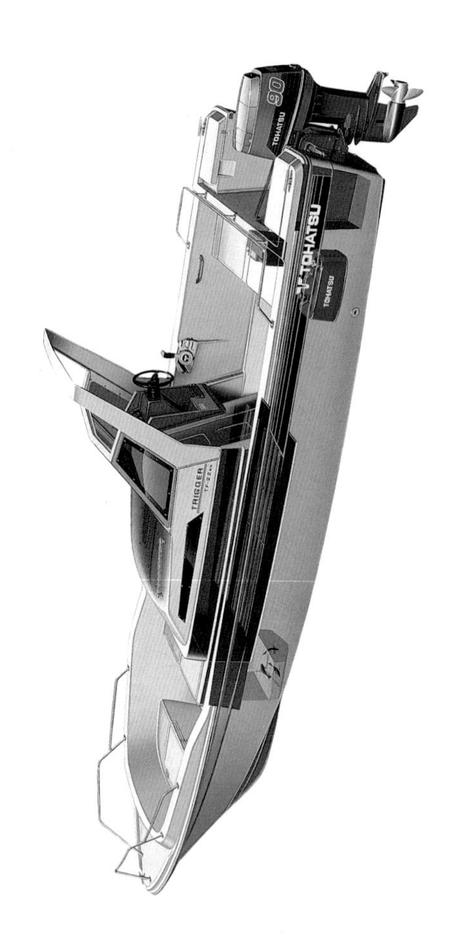

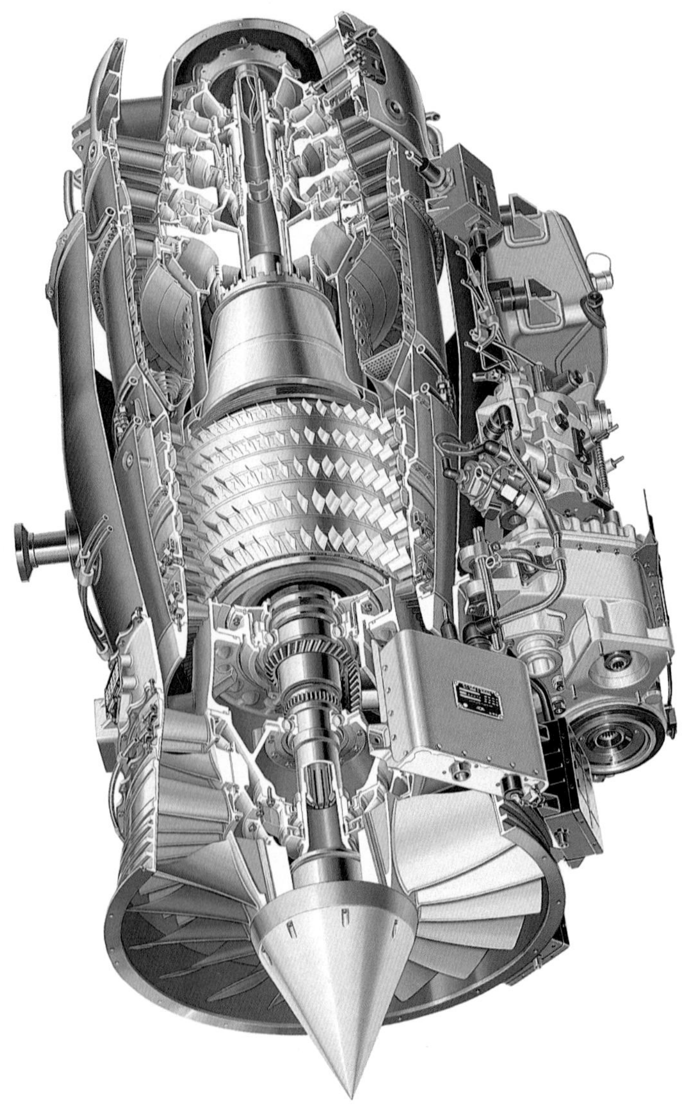

## JOHN SHELLEY

501-3-18-12 Shiroganedai
Minato-ku
Tokyo 108
Japan
Tel. 03-3443 8949
Fax: 03-3444 3198

18 Spinney Road
Thorpe St. Andrew Norwich
Norfolk NR7 0PW
United Kingdom
Tel. 0603-31585

**HITOSHI SHIBATA**

202 Jochi House
1-1-24 Hiroo
Shibuya-ku
Tokyo 150
Japan
Tel. 03-3499 1637

# HITOSHI SHIBATA

202 Jochi House
1-1-24 Hiroo
Shibuya-ku
Tokyo 150
Japan
Tel. 03-3499 1637

# HIROAKI SHIOYA

201 Frorie Hosoyama
751 Shinmaruko-cho
Nakahara-ku
Kawasaki City
Kanagawa 211
Japan
Tel. 044-733 3731
Fax: 044-733 3731

Agent:
POINT DELTA & ATY GROUP, INC.
Yasuhisa Azuma
295 Madison Ave., Suite # 926
New York, NY 10017
Tel. 212-949 7639
Fax: 212-949 7633

**KINTARO TAKAHASHI**

103 Chatelet Blanche
12-35 Sarugaku-cho
Shibuya-ku
Tokyo 150
Japan
Tel. 03-3476 2314

**MASAAKI TAKAUJI**

1007 Nakano Dai-2 Corpo
5-24-16 Nakano
Nakano-ku
Tokyo 164
Japan
Tel. 03-3228 6889

1007 Nakano Dai-2 Corpo
5-24-16 Nakano
Nakano-ku
Tokyo 164
Japan
Tel. 03-3228 6889

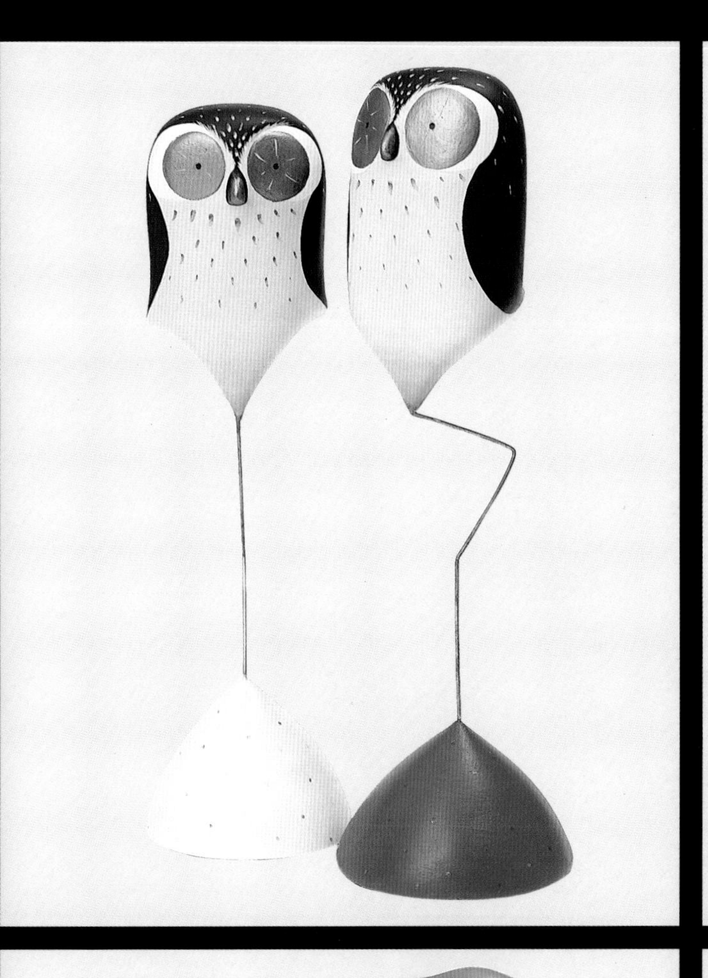

**TEN TOMISAWA**

3-84 Mukaikogane
Nagareyama City
Chiba 270-01
Japan
Tel. 0471-75 2282

# TSUKUSHI

305 Palaision Asagaya
1-6-7 Asagaya Minami
Suginami-ku
Tokyo 166
Japan
Tel. 03-3315 4592

**FUMIO WATANABE**
804 Konte Nishikasai
3-8-7 Nishikasai
Edogawa-ku
Tokyo 134
Japan
Tel. 03-3675 8526

# Illustrators

## Korea

## Corée

## Korea

Hosan Bldg. 2F. 709-8, Banpo-dong, Seocho-ku, Seoul, Korea, 137-040
Tel 02)512-3948, 3949/ Fax 02)512-3948

**"We are leaving for the most beautiful children's world with all the people in the world"**

It is our work to bring up dream to build children's open space and memorial open space at Panmunjom where north meets south to resolve military, ecnomic and political problem.

제2회
국제
그림동화
원화전
5.30→6.4


장 소
롯데백화점 본점 이벤트홀(8F)

주 최
대한출판문화협회

후 원
문화부
한국출판금고
한국출판미술가협회

협 찬
롯데백화점
웅진출판(주)

2nd
International Exhibition of
Picture Book Illustrations
for Children

China Cuba Czechoslovakia Fiji France India Iran Italy Japan Korea Nigeria Soviet Sudan Thiland

1. For Contribution toward cultural exchanges between nations and making good fridens with each other, we try to play our roll through arranging exhibitions and concerts, etc.

2. For the Future, we prepared a meeting "Let's think Tomorrow". We discussed present and future circumstances with experts invited from inside and outside the country, so as to be good friends for the future.

3. For Raising a fund which will be spend in future for children in great necessity in Asian-pacific Areas, we are spreading saving boxes to be opended at 20:00 Feb. 20th at dawn of 21st centry, 2000.

4. For Establishing library of educationals, We are gathering children's picture books, book about music and play for children, donated by friends working in every fields in Asian-Pacific areas.

5. For Children's Picture Book of their Mother's own making, we are introducing the way to make them and how to help children develop emotional and intellectual ability.

6. For Cooperation with public bodies, artists, designers and musicians in various cultural events etc., we provide suggestions and helping hands in doing creative works to get new opportunities in life.

**HANIL DESIGN**

Dae Sung Bldg # 502
48-4, Choongmooro, 2 Ga
Joong-gu
Seoul
Korea
Tel. 02-266 5140
275 7410

## HART WORK / HUH SANG-HOE

Zip 100-271
Room No. 502 Donghwa Bldg
43-1 Pil-Dong, 1-Ga
1, Chung-gu
Seoul
Korea
Tel. 02-272 6971

Clients:
Oricom Ad. Co., Inc. - L.G. Ad. Co., Inc. - Samheui Ad. Co., Inc. - Geumgang Ad. Co., Inc. - Daehong Ad. Co., Inc. - Daebang Ad. Co., Inc. - Hanin Ad. Co., Inc. - Dongbang Ad. Co., Inc. - KAL - Yongin Farmland.

We have worked since 1980.
Our main field is the extremely realistic illustration with airbrush for advertising.

Original Work *Uranus's ice ring* by Huh, Sang-Hoe

*Lecaf* Golden Sale Poster by Ryu, Jae-Gon

Advertisement of the enterprise of Jinro

*Doosan Ginseng-D*
Newspaper Ad. & Poster

*Chopstick*
Magazine Ad.

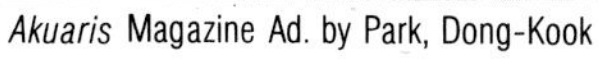

*Akuaris* Magazine Ad. by Park, Dong-Kook

Advertisement of the enterprise of Hyeondae by Jang, Jun-Hee

*Ramada Renaissance Hotel* Magazine Ad. by Kim, Jin-Ho

*La La Sense* Magazine Ad.

## KANG WOO-HYON

Cross Cultural Center for Asia
Hosan Bldg, 2F
709-8, Banpo-Dong
Seocho-ku
Seoul 137 040
Korea
Tel. 02-512 3948
512 3949
Fax: 02-512 3948

Agent:
Cross Cultural Center for Asia
Hosan Bldg, 2F
709-8, Banpo-Dong
Seochou-ku
Seoul 137 040
Korea

# KIM EUN-JOO

114-208 Sinbanpo — 5th Apt.
Jam Won Dong
Seoch-Ku
Seoul
Korea
Tel. 02-584 7262

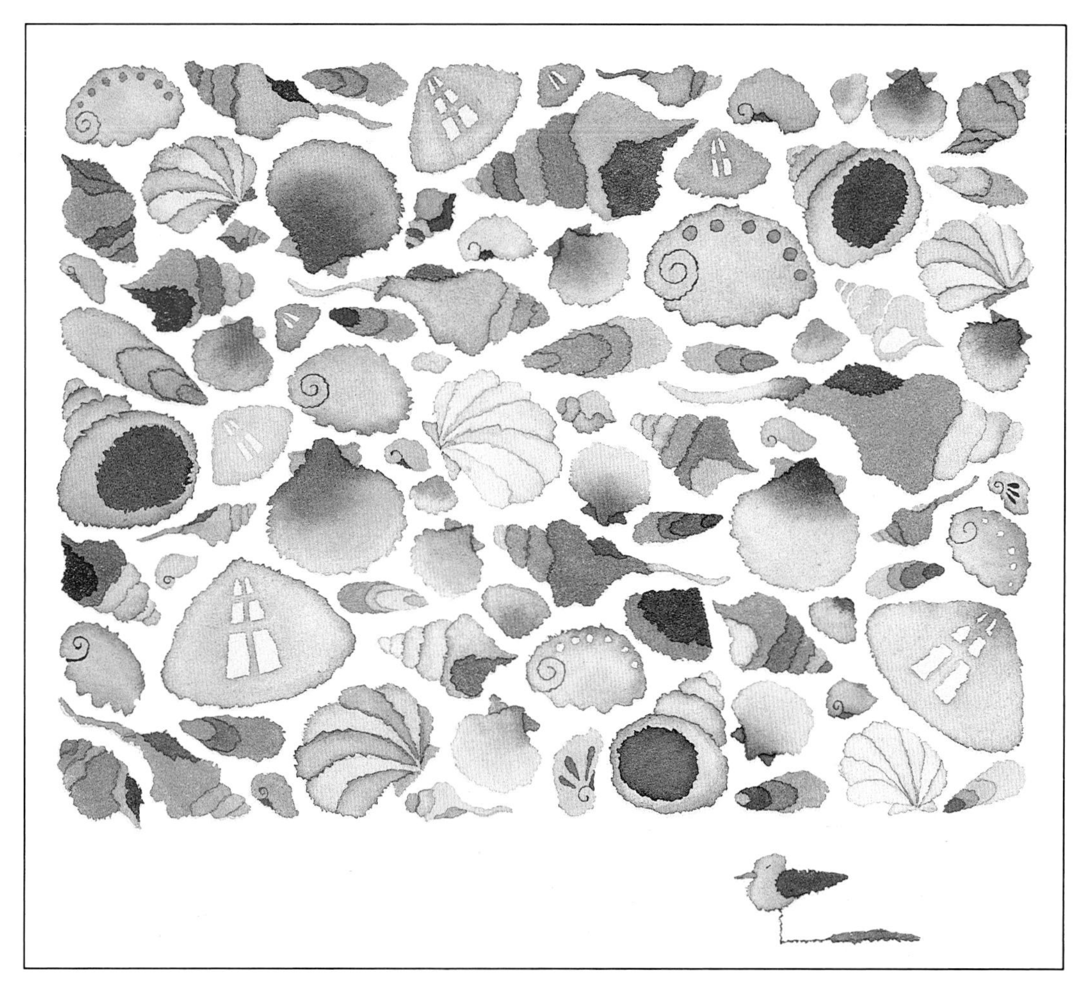

## LEE BOK-SHIK

160, Kil-Dong
Kang Dong-ku
Seoul
Korea
Tel. 02-485 6385

Received a BA in sculpture from Hong-Ik University.
Joined the Jeil Advertising Co.
Worked as a freelance illustrator.

Received a prize from the Choong-Ang Daily News Advertising Contest in Illustration.

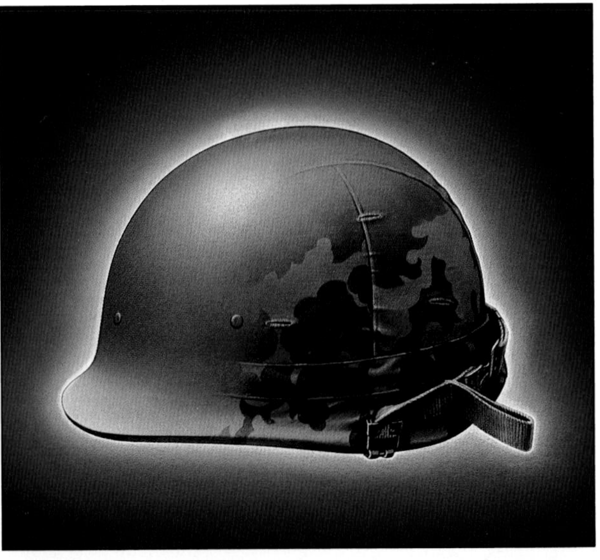

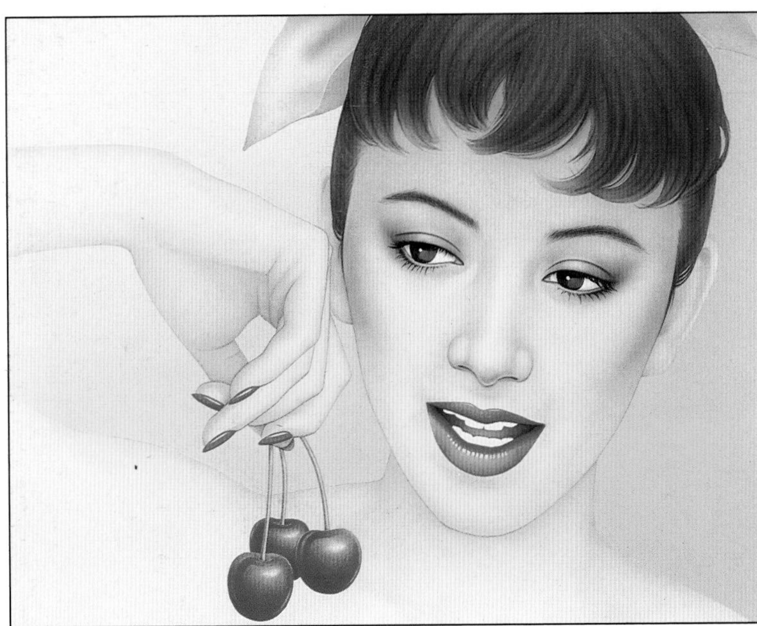

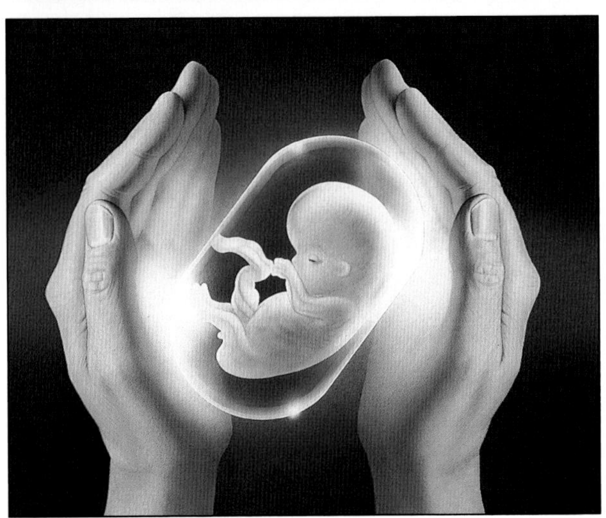

## LEE HAERY

17-25, Sibum Apt.
Yeoido-Dong
Youngdungpo-gu
Seoul
Korea
Tel. 02-782 4147

Has written for and illustrated a children's magazine "BOBA BOBA" series.
Currently working as a freelance illustrator, illustrating magazines and picture books.

137-069 Sang-A BD, 2133 Bang Bae-Dong, Seocho-Gu, Seoul, Korea.
Tel. 02-591 8463 / 02-591 7565. Fax: 02-591 7565.

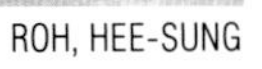

ROH, HEE-SUNG

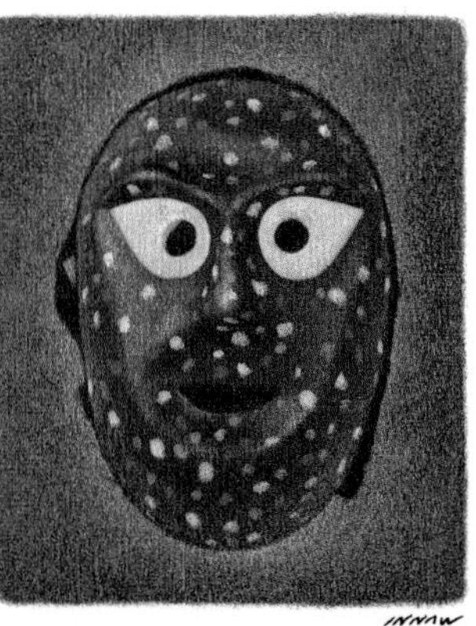

ROH, HEE-SUNG

LEE, CHUN-GIL

OH, YOU-KYUNG

ROH, HEE-SUNG

LEE, JU-YONG

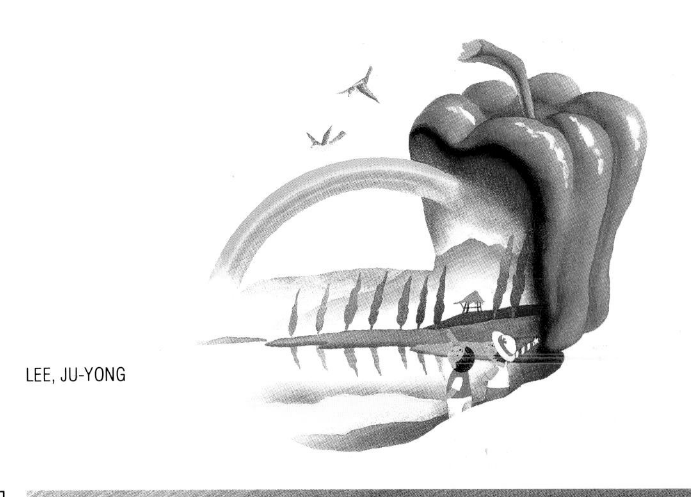

OH, YOU-KYUNG

SUNG, SANG-WON

**LEE JOON-SUP**

330-36, Sukyo-Dong
Mapo-ku
Seoul
Korea
Tel. 02-337 0360

## LIU JAE-SOO

Hosan Bldg, 2F
709-8, Banpo-Dong
Seocho-ku
Seoul 137 040
Korea
Tel. 02-512 3948
512 3949
543 9853
Fax: 02-512 3948

## LEE SUNG-PYO

407-1407, Chugong Apt.
Kwachon
Kyongki-do
Korea
Tel. 02-502 9607

## OUK KANG-CHANG

254-10, Shin Hun Dong
Seo-gu
In Chun
Korea
Tel. 032-572 1915


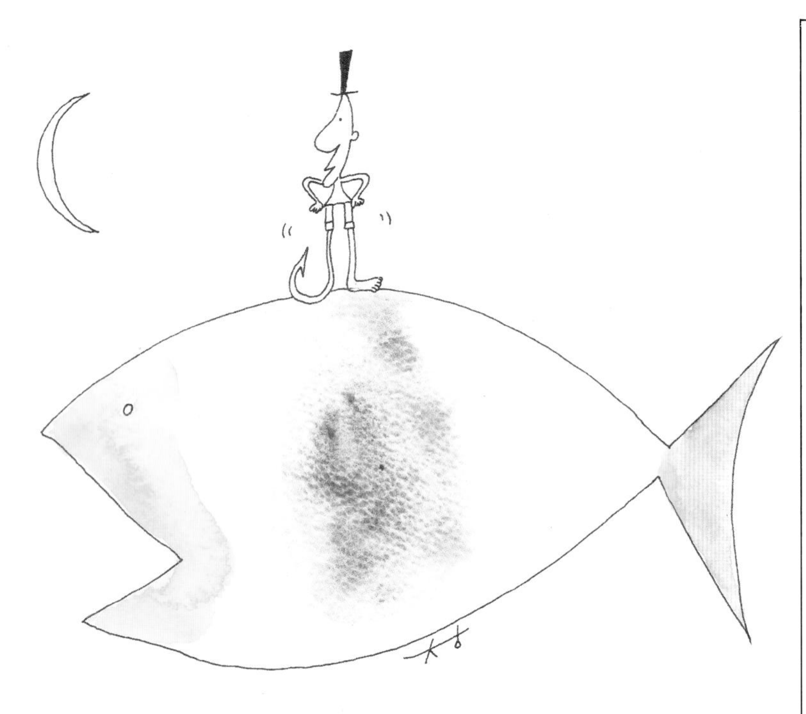

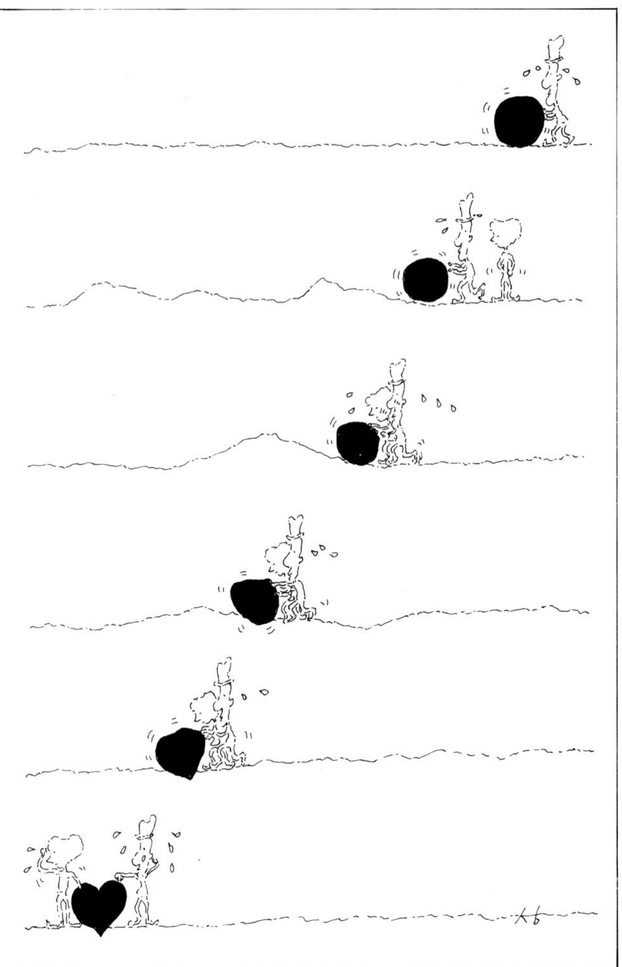

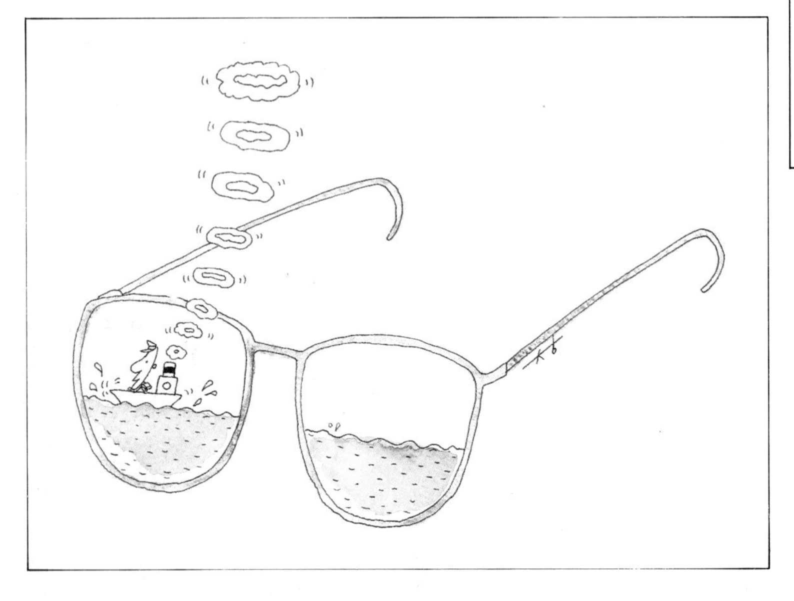

# RHIE WON-BOK

Song-pa
Shinchun 7
Jangmi A. 14-1407
Seoul 134 240
Korea
Tel. 02-422 1256

Seoul National University
Uni. MÜNSTER / W. GERMANY
PROFESSOR / DUKSUNG WOMEN'S UNI.
Dept. of Visual Communication.

Bookcover of
"The Capitalism & The Communism"

"Netherland"
One of the 12 pictures "The Europe"

# Illustrators

# Malaysia
# Malaisie
# Malaysia

# CREATIVE ENTERPRISE SDN. BHD.

JAAFAR TAIB

38 Jalan 1/82B
Bangsar Utama
59000 Kuala Lumpur
Malaysia
Tel. 03-230 49 70
Fax: 03-230 49 67

Colour Separation C.H. COLOUR SCAN.

# CREATIVE ENTERPRISE SDN. BHD.

ZAINAL BUANG HUSSEIN

38 Jalan 1/82B
Bangsar Utama
59000 Kuala Lumpur
Malaysia
Tel. 03-230 49 70
Fax: 03-230 49 67

Colour Separation C.H. COLOUR SCAN.

# CREATIVE ENTERPRISE SDN. BHD.

AZMAN YUSOF

38 Jalan 1/82B
Bangsar Utama
59000 Kuala Lumpur
Malaysia
Tel. 03-230 49 70
Fax: 03-230 49 67

Colour Separation C.H. COLOUR SCAN.

# CREATIVE ENTERPRISE SDN. BHD.

38 Jalan 1/82B
Bangsar Utama
59000 Kuala Lumpur
Malaysia
Tel. 03-230 49 70
Fax: 03-230 49 67

JAAFAR TAIB

REJABHAD

UJANG

ZUNAR

CABAI

AMAN

LI

LONG Colour Separation C.H. COLOUR SCAN.

# CREATIVE ENTERPRISE SDN. BHD.

38 Jalan 1/82B
Bangsar Utama
59000 Kuala Lumpur
Malaysia
Tel. 03-230 49 70
Fax: 03-230 49 67

AZA — KULAT — JAAFAR TAIB — NOT — ROSLIM — FATAH — KERENGGE — ROY — RODIN — BOY P.J.

Colour Separation C.H. COLOUR SCAN.

# Illustrators

# Australia
# Australie
# Australien

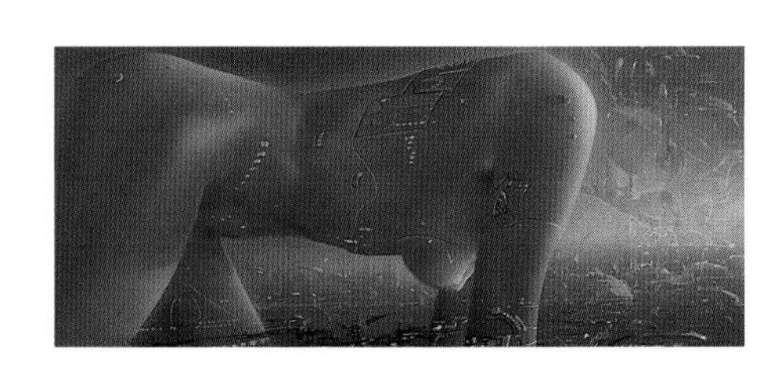

G R E G O R Y

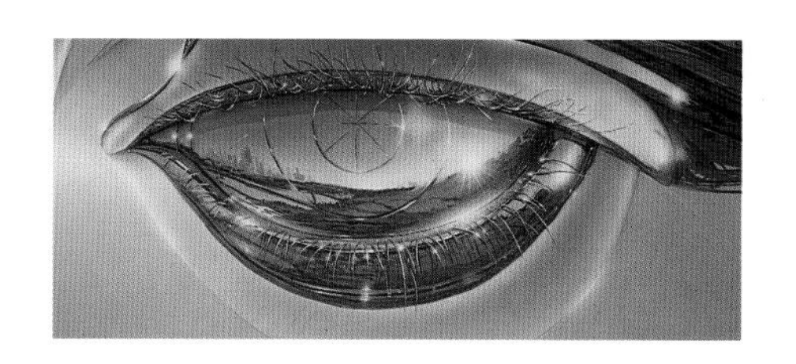

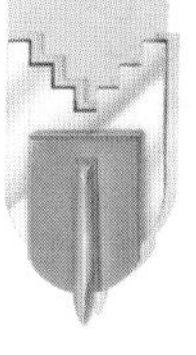

FUTURISTIC

AX [02]636 5245

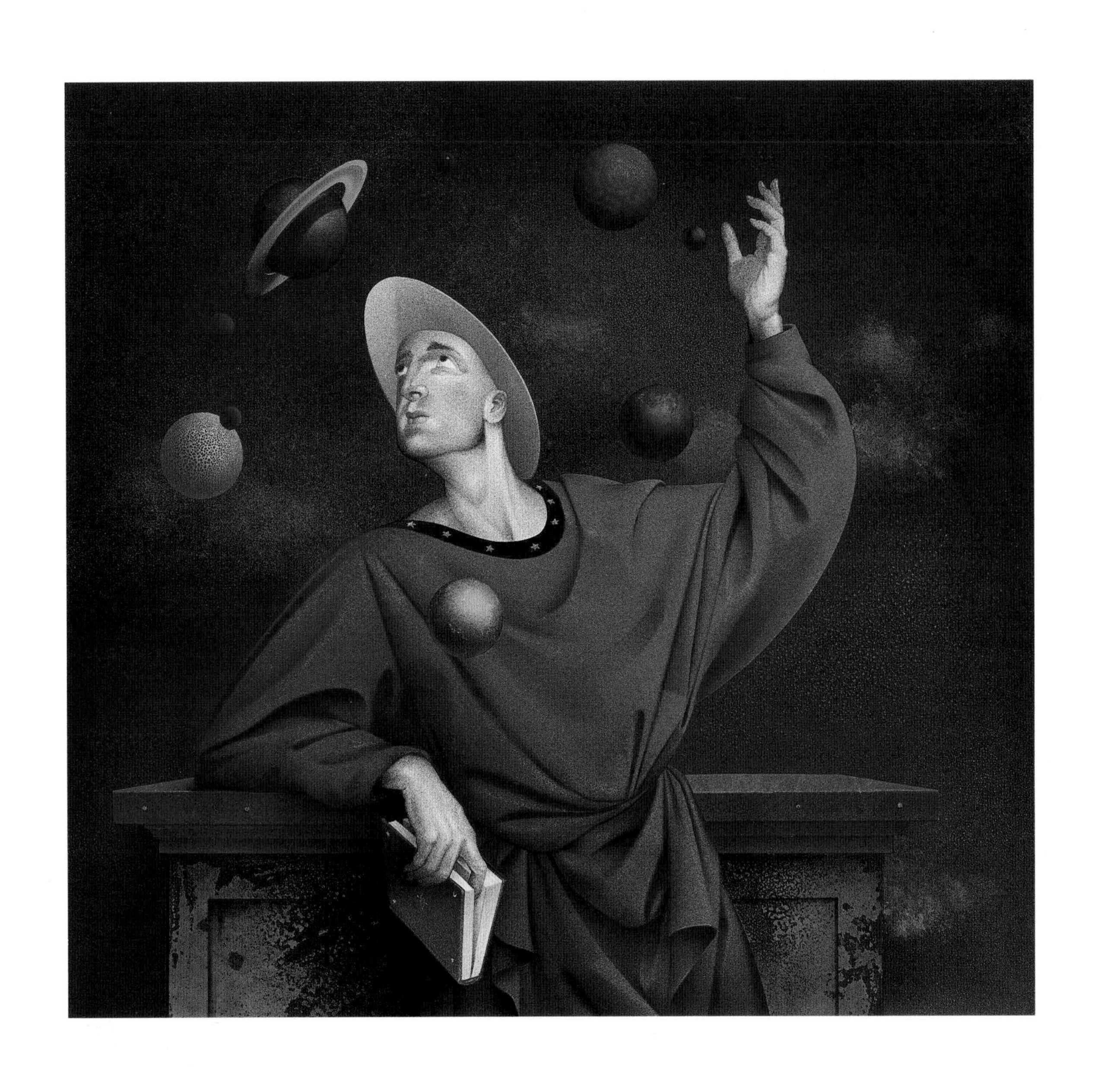

NIGEL BUCHANAN 243 RILEY STREET SURRY HILLS SYDNEY NSW 2010 TELEPHONE (02) 211 1396

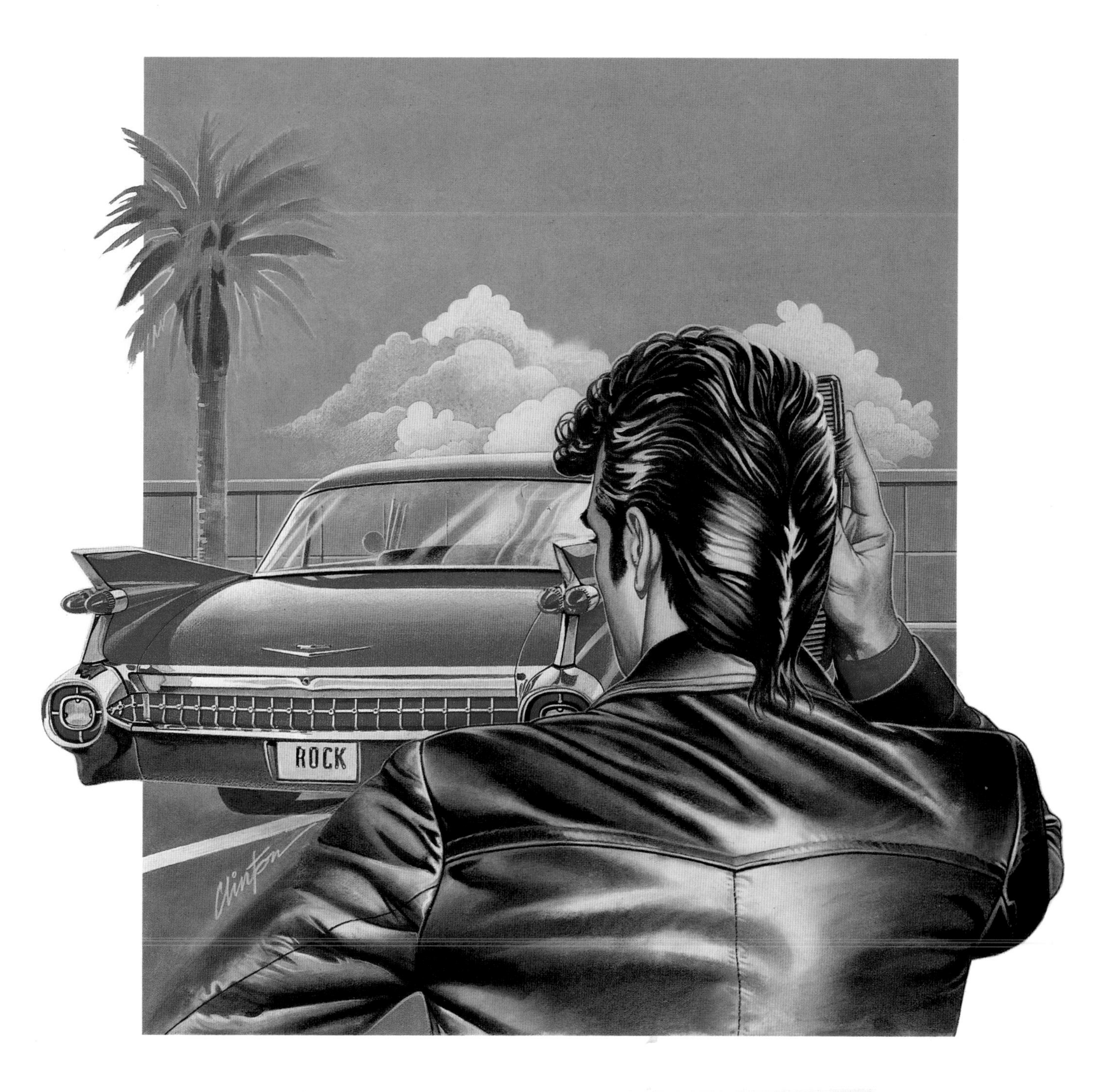


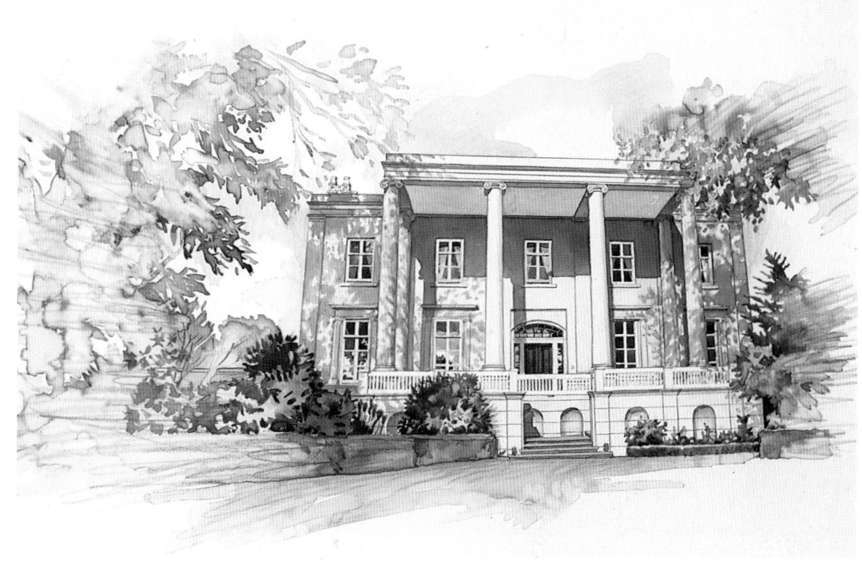

**BRIAN CLINTON**

Brian Clinton & Assoc. 2 Karjen Place, Wheelers Hill, Melbourne, Victoria 3150
☐ 03) 560 4351 Fax 03) 560 4351

**GEOFF COOK**
752 Inkerman Road, North Caulfield, Melbourne, Victoria 3161
☐ 03) 509 3919 Fax: 03) 500 0556

**DIANNE GAMESON**
196 Nelson Road, South Melbourne, Victoria 3205 ☐ 03) 699 1571

**DIANNE GAMESON**
196 Nelson Road, South Melbourne, Victoria 3205 ☐ 03) 699 1571

**MIKE GOLDING**
Level 5. 24/38 Bellevue Street, Surry Hills, Sydney, New South Wales 2010.
☐ 02) 211 2243 Fax: 02) 281 1632

**CRAIG McGILL**
Unit 10.6 Hughenden Road, East St Kilda, Victoria 3182
☐ 03) 527 5234 Fax 03) 527 6106

**BARRY OLIVE**
ILLUSTRATION
PTY LTD
G5, 283 ALFRED
STREET NORTH
NORTH SYDNEY
NSW 2060
**PH 02 957 5598**

MARGARET POWER

Illustrations • Storyboards
Visuals • Fashion

Flat Six, 6 Sidwell Avenue,
East St. Kilda, Victoria 3182.
☐ 03) 527 4330

EUROLYNX LTD.

EUROLYNX LTD.

EUROLYNX LTD.

NATIONAL AUSTRALIA BANK.

**CHANTAL STEWART**
15 Denver Crescent, Elsternwick, Melbourne, Victoria 3185 ☐ 03) 528 1494

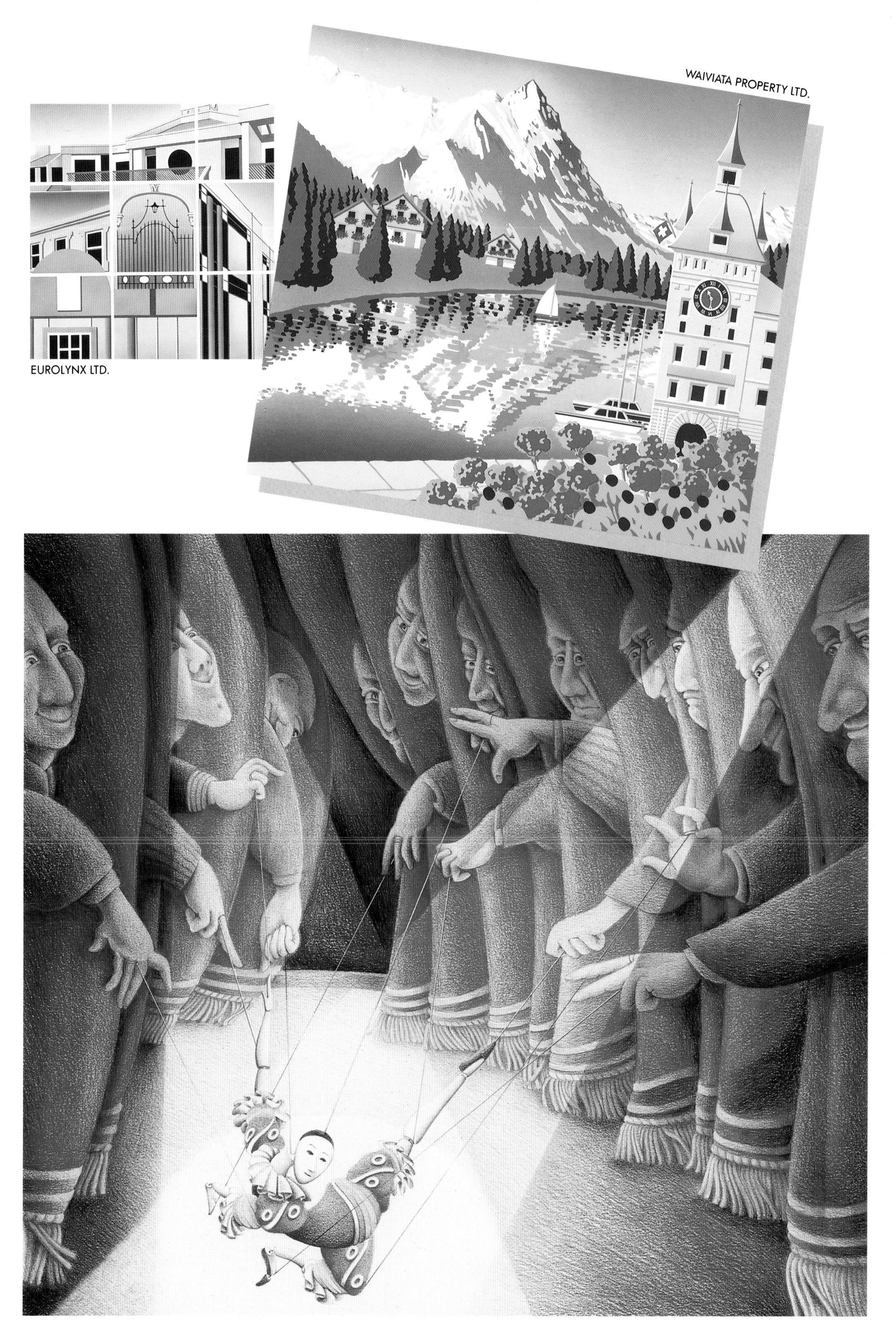

WAIVIATA PROPERTY LTD.

EUROLYNX LTD.

NATIONAL AUSTRALIA BANK.

**CHANTAL STEWART**

15 Denver Crescent, Elsternwick, Melbourne, Victoria 3185 ☐ 03) 528 1494

# GENEVIEVE REES ILLUSTRATION

Illustration, Visuals, Storyboards
1 Cecil Place, Prahran, Victoria 3181
Telephone 529 5579 • Fax 525 1512

# Illustrators

# Austria
# Autriche
# Österreich

**WOLFGANG RIEDER**

Lienfeldergasse 54/6-7
A-1160 Wien
Tel. 0222-45 17 673

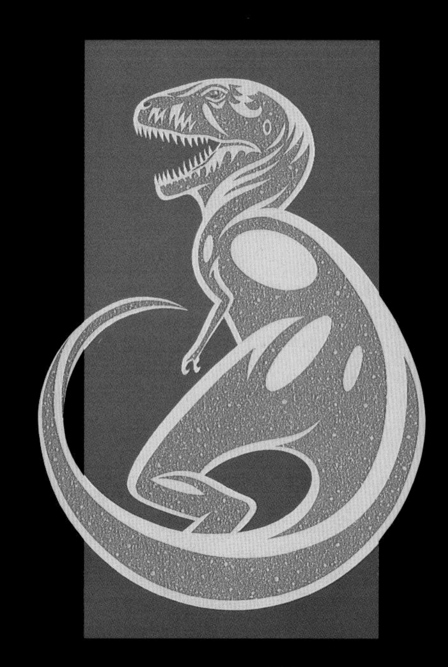

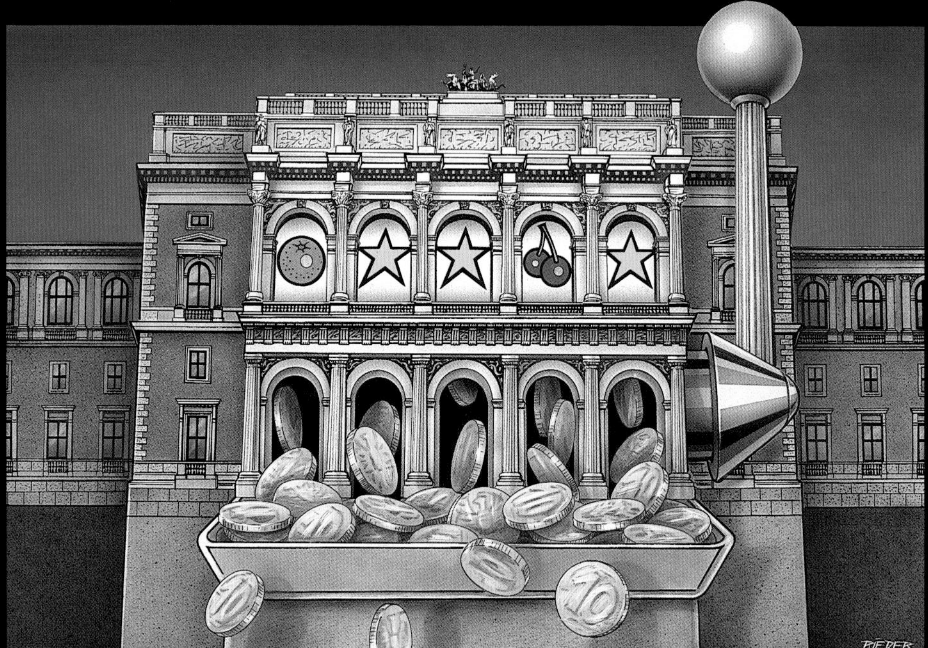

Lienfeldergasse 54/6-7
A-1160 Wien
Tel. 0222-45 17 673

PLEESZ MICHAEL · A-1060 WIEN · WINDMÜHLGASSE 25/6 · TEL.: 587 37 80

# Illustrators

## Germany
## Allemagne
## Deutschland

## VOLKMAR RINKE

Albertus-Magnus-Strasse 55
D-3200 Hildesheim
Tel. 05121-26 30 10

Illustrator and graphic designer with long years of experience.
Diversified in technics and styles.
Always interested in new works for advertising agencies, editors, and creative directors.

Illustrator und Grafikdesigner mit langjähriger Erfahrung.
Vielseitig in Technik und Stilrichtung.
Immer an neuer Aufgaben von Werbeagenturen, Verlagen und Werbetreibenden interessiert.

Illustrateur et dessinateur-graphiste de longue expérience.
Diversité dans les techniques et les styles.
Toujours intéressé par de nouveaux travaux pour agences de publicité, éditeurs et publicitaires.

# TECHNICAL ART GmbH

NORBERT SCHÄFER
LUDWIG EBERL

Dreieichstrasse 50
D-6057 Dietzenbach
Tel. 06074-25033
25081
Fax: 06074-25033

Branch:
Press and advertising.

Speciality:
Hyperrealistic illustration.

Strengths:
All technical representations and production with colour cuts or phantom-illustration.

Arbeitsbereich:
Presse und Werbung.

Spezialgebiet:
Hyperrealistische Illustrationen.

Schwerpunkte:
Alle technischen Darstellungen und Funktionsabläufe als Farbschnitt-oder Phantom-Illustration.

Major clients / Wichtige Kunden:
Audi, BMW, Buderus, KHD, Ford, Opel, Leitz, MBB, Porsche, SKF, u.a. & Agenturen.

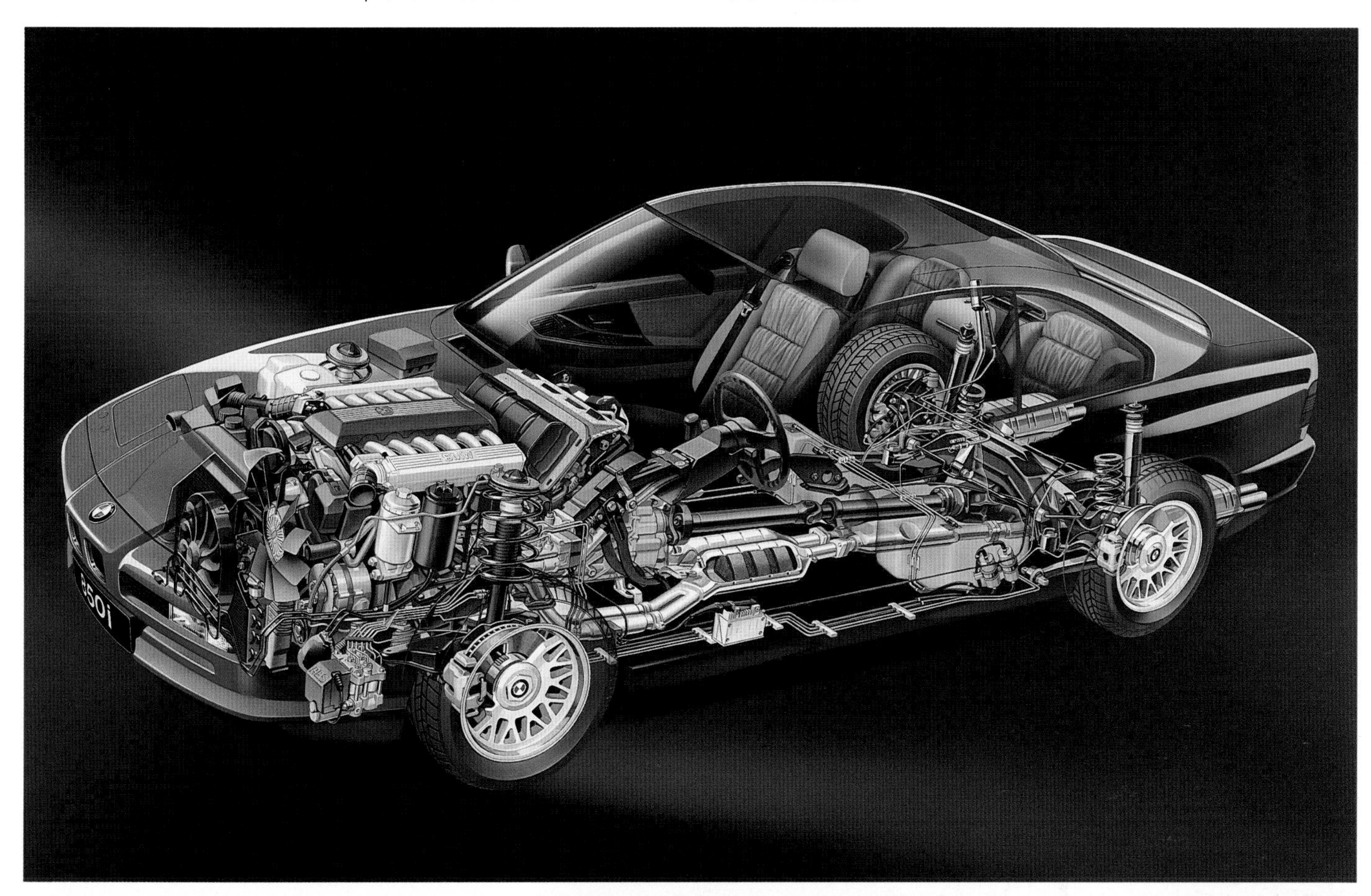


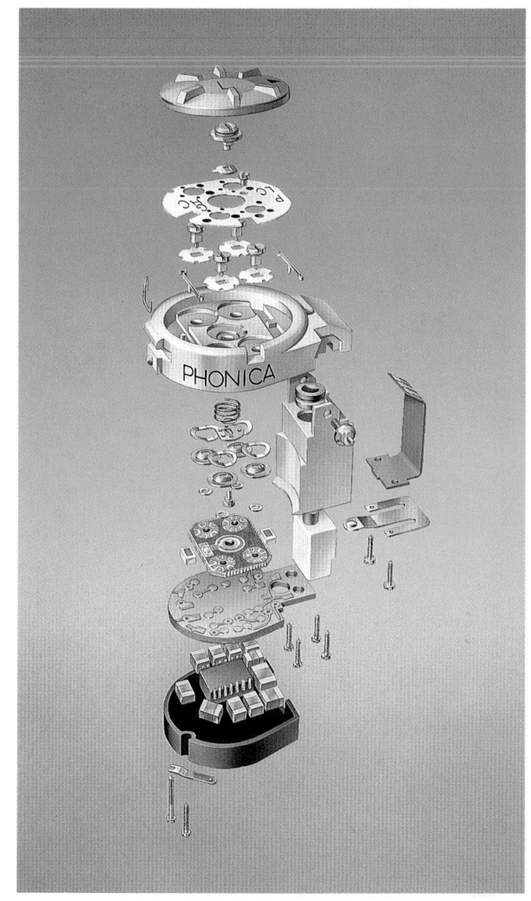


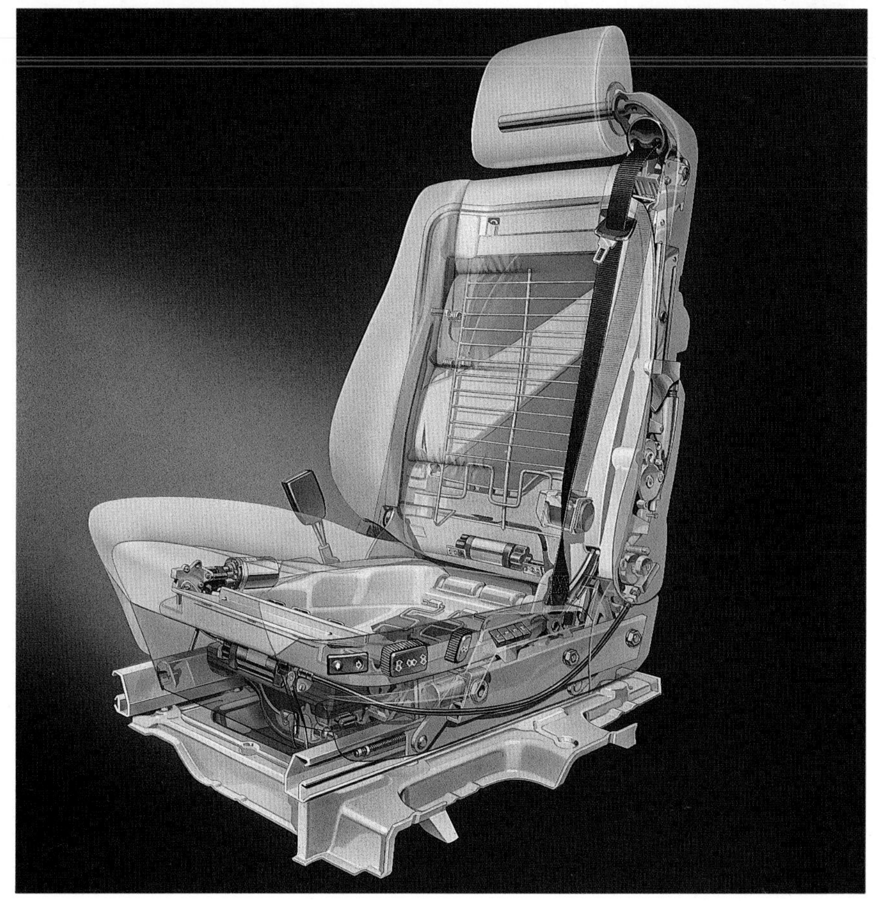

# GEERT BORDICH

Eschenweg 3
D-2082 Tornesch
Tel. 04122-5 21 51

Agent:
GUDRUN TEMPELMANN-BOEHR
Am Rosenbaum 7
D-4006 Erkrath
Tel. 0211-25 32 46

Illustration and graphic design in various technics and styles.

Illustration und Grafik in verschiedenen Techniken und Stilrichtungen.

Illustration et graphisme dans divers techniques et styles.

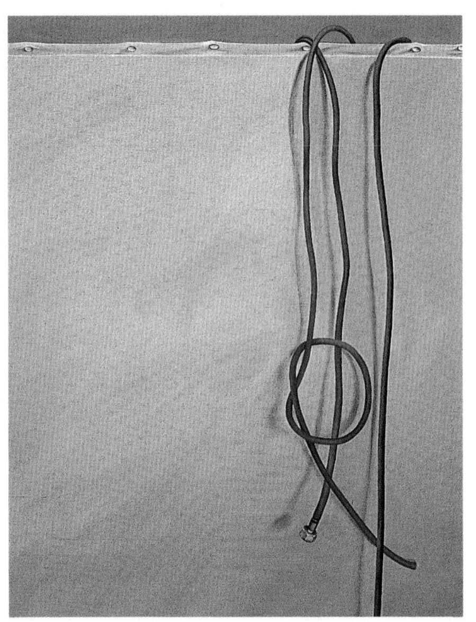

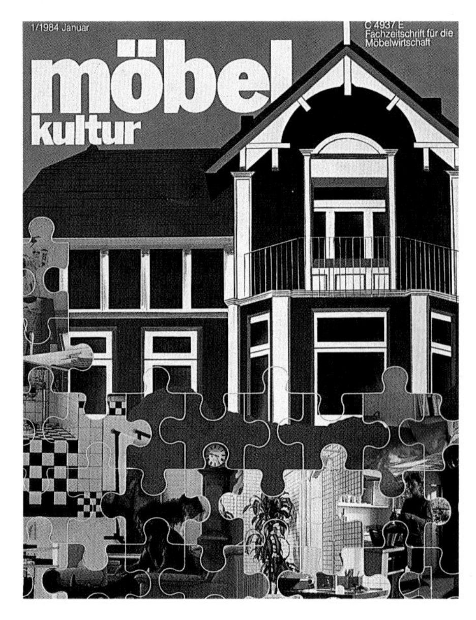

# ERIKA MOOS-DREVENSTEDT

Paul-Gerhardt-Strasse 23
D-4156 Willich 2 - Anrath
Tel. 02156-3806 - Fax: 02156-1380

Illustrations:
figurative, plants, caricature, layout, storyboards.

Illustration:
Figürliches, Pflanzen, Karikatur, Layout, Storyboards.

Illustrations:
figuratives, plantes, caricatures, maquettes, storyboards.

# ARI PLIKAT

Steinmetzstrasse 13
D-4600 Dortmund
Tel. 0231-51 52 27
Fax: 0231-51 59 17

Represented by:
Mrs. Gudrun Tempelmann-Boehr
Agentur für Fotografen und
Illustratoren
Am Rosenbaum 7
D-4006 Erkrath 1
Tel. 0211-25 32 46
Fax: 0211-25 46 32

# URSZULA KOREJWO

Borstellstrasse 36
D-1000 Berlin 41
Tel. 030-219 000 72
Fax: 030-219 000 71


Interior and exterior architecture – demonstration pictures of still inexistent objects.
Technical illustration of all kind.
Fantasy pictures.
Airbrush, oil, pencil, mixed technic.

Innen- und Aussenarchitektur – Schaubilder von noch nicht entstandenen Objekten.
Technische Illustrationen aller Art.
Fantasiebilder.
Airbrush, Öl, Bleistift, Mischtechnik.

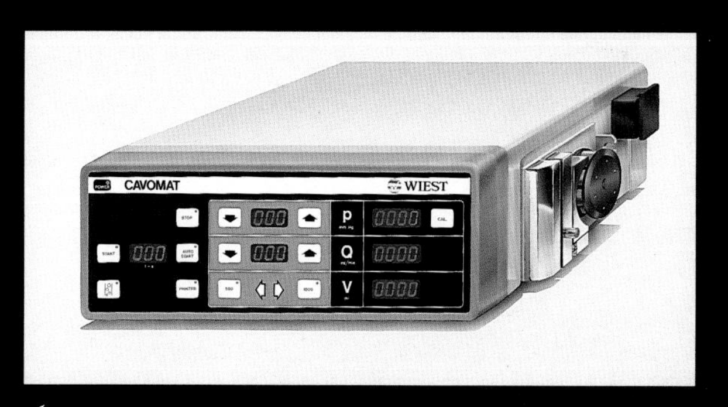

## FRANK GERHARDT

Johannisstrasse 36
D-4800 Bielefeld 1
Tel. 0521-87 43 88
Fax: 0521- 8 61 15

In few words:
- LINIE-Grafik.
- Illustration for advertising and newspapers.
- Various technics.
- From comic to photorealism.
- Catalogue free of charge on request.

In Stichworten:
- LINIE-Grafik.
- Illustrationen für Werbung und Zeitschriften.
- Vielzahl von Techniken.
- Von Comic bis Fotorealismus.
- Katalog kostenlos anfordern.

En quelques mots:
- LINIE-Grafik.
- Illustrations pour publicité et journaux.
- Techniques diverses.
- De la bande dessinée à la photo réaliste.
- Catalogue gratuit sur demande.

# STEPHAN WOHLGEMUTH

Steinle Strasse 32
D-6000 Frankfurt 70
Tel. 069-631 38 72

You see what you get.

# ALBERT-ERICH MAIER

Mühlgasse 8
D-7959 Unterbalzheim
Tel. 07347-7165
Fax: 07347-7919

Illustration, graphic design, retouch. Technics, nature and fantaisy.

Illustration, Grafik, Retusche. Technik, Natur, Fantasy.

Illustration, graphisme, retouches. Techniques, nature et fantaisie.

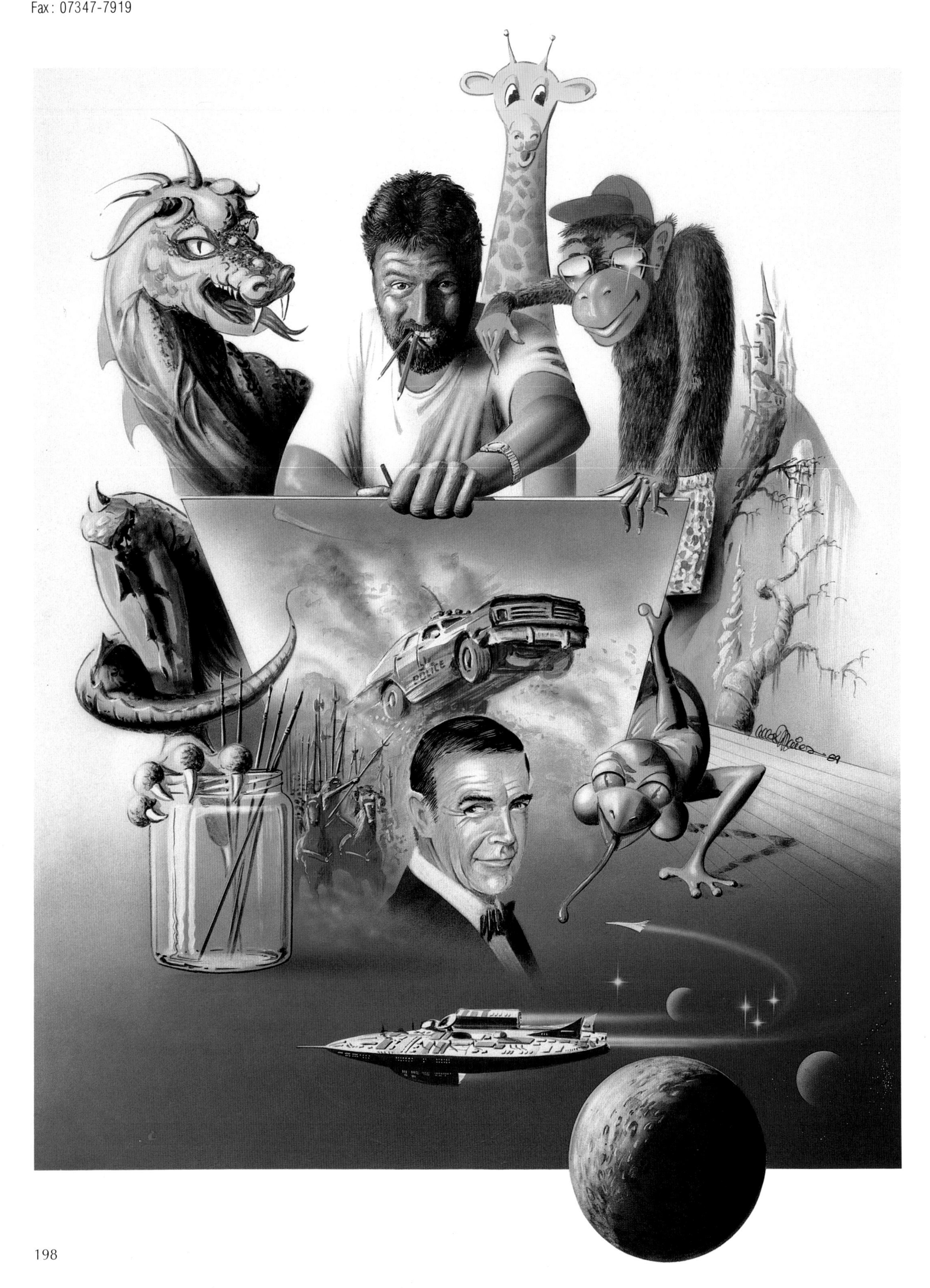

## ANDRÉ ROCHE

Katharinenstraße 10
D-8000 München 71
Tel. 089- 79 50 15
Fax: 089-791 78 59

Specialised since 1975 in authentic reproduction of existing designs which are under licence for marketing. Creates and optimises well-known advertising characters. Transformation of 2D-figures into 3D-figures. Comic strips, airbrush-illustrations, animatics and full production of animated cartoons.

Seit 1975 Spezialist für unverfälschte Wiedergabe des original-Zeichenstils bei der Umsetzung von Lizenzfiguren. Kreation von Werbefiguren. Optimierung vorhandenes Figurendesigns. 3D-Umsetzung von 2D-Figuren. Comics, Cartoons, Airbrush-Illustrationen, Animatics, Trickfilm-Vollproduktion.

Spécialisé depuis 1975 dans la reproduction authentique de dessins, existant déjà sous licence commerciale. Création et optimisation de personnages publicitaires. Transforme les images à 2 dimensions en modèle à 3 dimensions. Bandes dessinées, illustration à l'aérographe, animatics et production complète de dessins animés.

"the best licensed-characters-designer in Germany"* also creates new heroes!

*(Medien Bulletin 9/89)

# UWE HURLEBAUS

DIPL.-DESIGNER FH

Gaildorfer Strasse 80
D-7157 Murrhardt 2
Tel. 07192-5155
Fax: 07192-1666

Agent:
G. Tempelmann-Boehr
Am Rosenbaum 7
D-4006 Erkrath 1
Tel. 0211-25 32 46

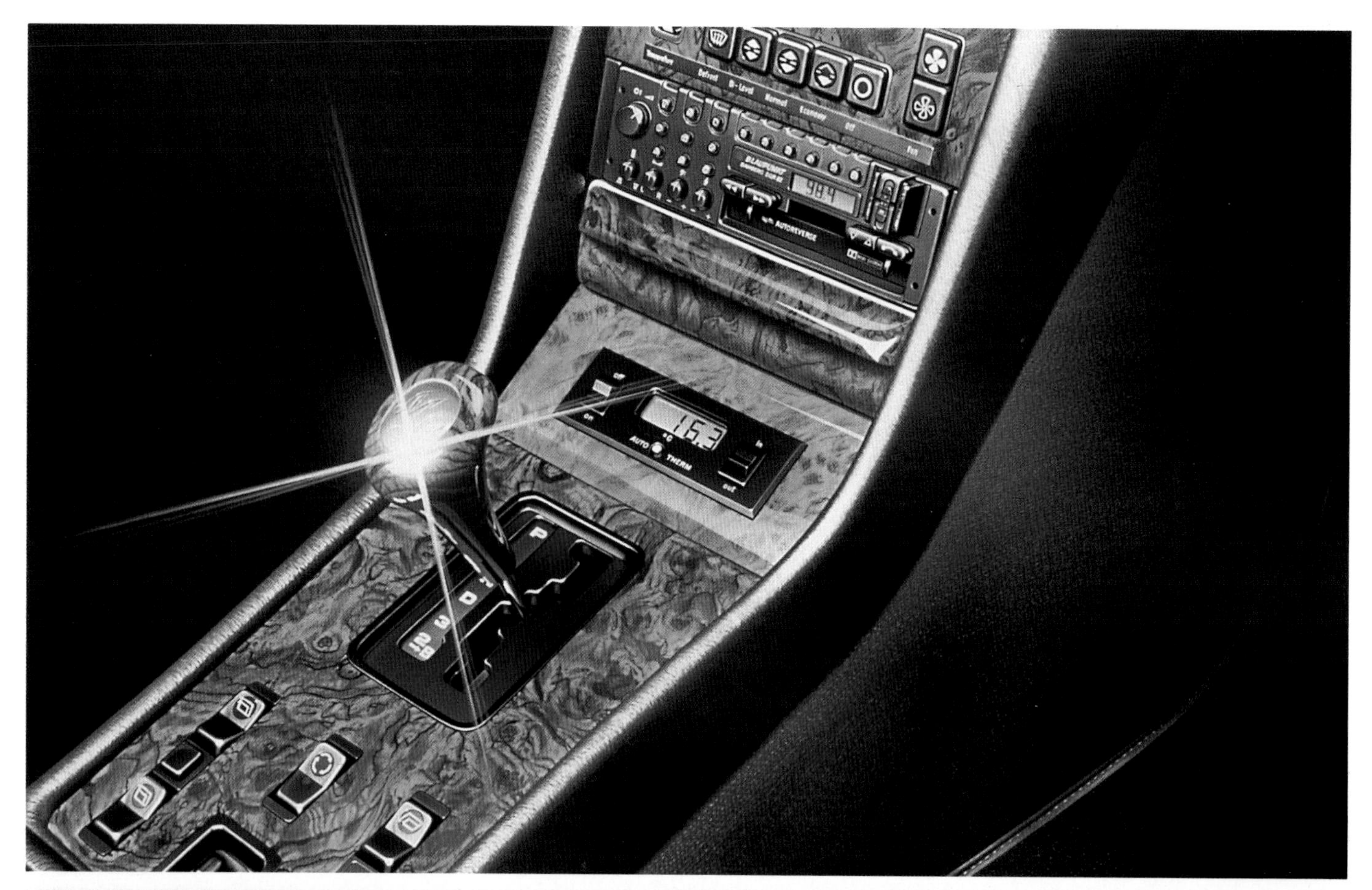

# UWE HURLEBAUS

DIPL.-DESIGNER FH

Gaildorfer Strasse 80
D-7157 Murrhardt 2
Tel. 07192-5155
Fax: 07192-1666

Agent:
G. Tempelmann-Boehr
Am Rosenbaum 7
D-4006 Erkrath 1
Tel. 0211-25 32 46

# WILLY GILTMANN – CLAUS DIERCKS

Art & Werbeteam GmbH

Borselstr. 3
2000 Hamburg 50
Tel. 040-390 79 72/73/74
Fax: 040-390 79 75

Was immer Sie wollen:
Bilder, Ideen, Visionen, Illustrationen!

**VOLKER HILBEL**

DIPL. DESIGNER (FH)
Kronwinklerstr. 24
D-8000 München 60
Tel. 089-863 24 22
Fax: 089-863 24 71

Conception.
Art direction.
Illustration.
Computer graphic.

Konzeption.
Art-Direction.
Illustration.
Computergrafik.

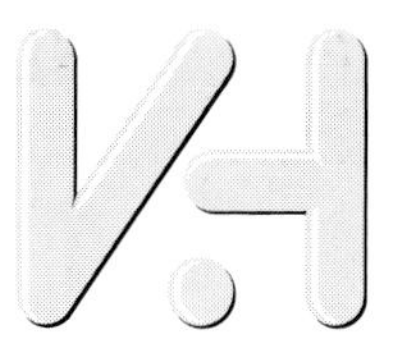

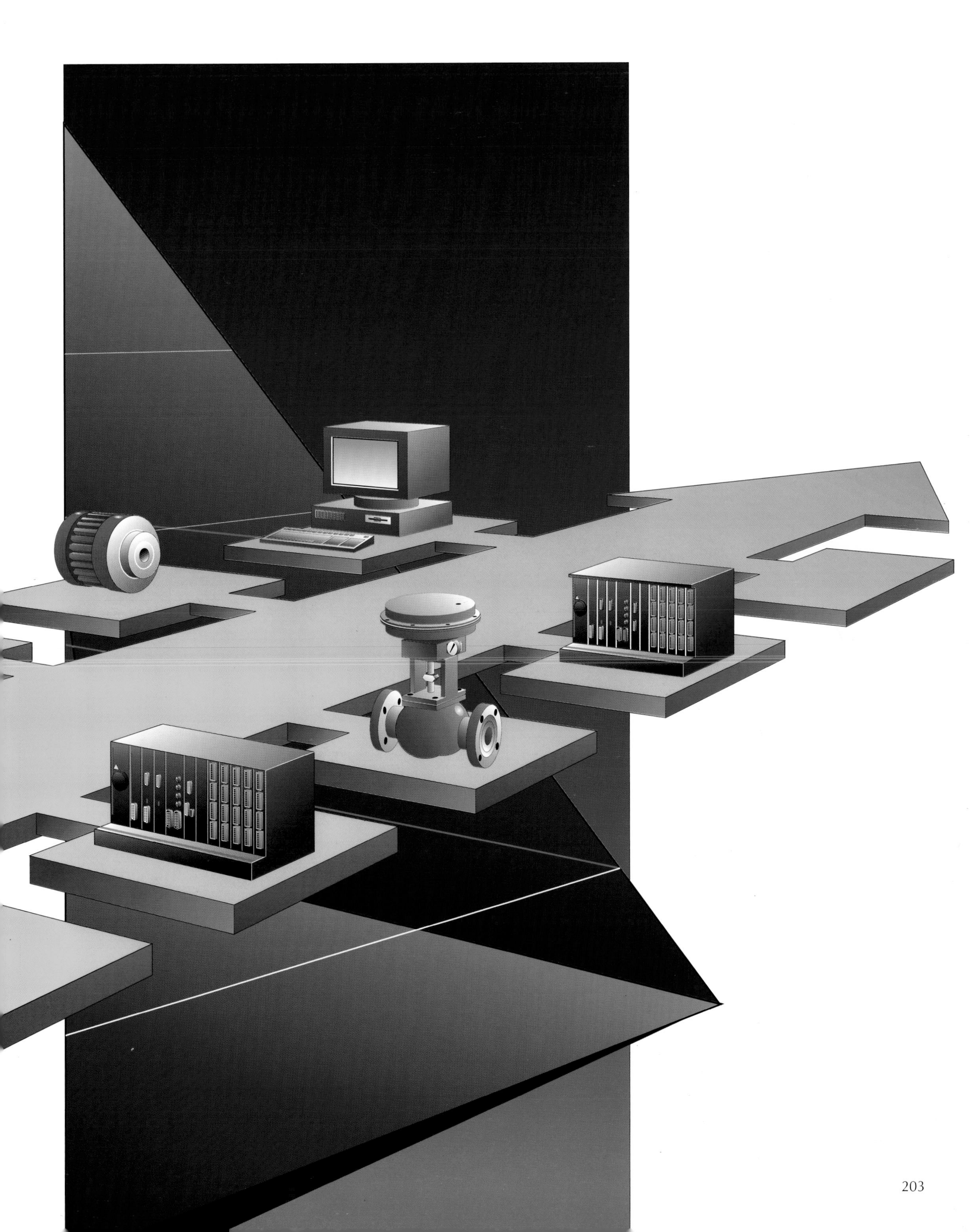

## SIGI WIND

Eichendorffstrasse 43
D-8012 Ottobrunn
Tel. 089-609 04 61
Fax: 089-609 05 62

Illustration, graphic design and painting in mixed technics.
Airbrush and applied works for private, advertising agencies and editors.

Illustration, Grafikdesign und Malerei in Mischtechnik.
Airbrush und angewandte Arbeiten für Privat, Werbeagenturen und Verlage.

Illustration, graphisme et peinture en techniques mixtes.
Aérographe et travaux appliqués pour privés, agences de publicité, éditeurs.

# Illustrators

## Switzerland
## Suisse
## Schweiz

# THIERRY CLAUSON

Rue des Eaux-Vives 27
CH-1207 Genève
Tel. 022-736 65 10
Fax: 022-736 65 10

Clients include / Kunden:
Carré Noir, Heinz Heimann Unicom, Saatchy & Saatchy, McCann-Erickson, HDM, Bozell, Mahogany, Fides, The Image Bank, RotoVision, Département de la Culture Genève, Macao.

# THIERRY CLAUSON

Rue des Eaux-Vives 27
CH-1207 Genève
Tel. 022-736 65 10
Fax: 022-736 65 10

Clients include / Kunden:
Carré Noir, Heinz Heimann Unicom, Saatchy & Saatchy, McCann-Erickson, HDM, Bozell, Mahogany, Fides, The Image Bank, RotoVision, Département de la Culture Genève, Macao.

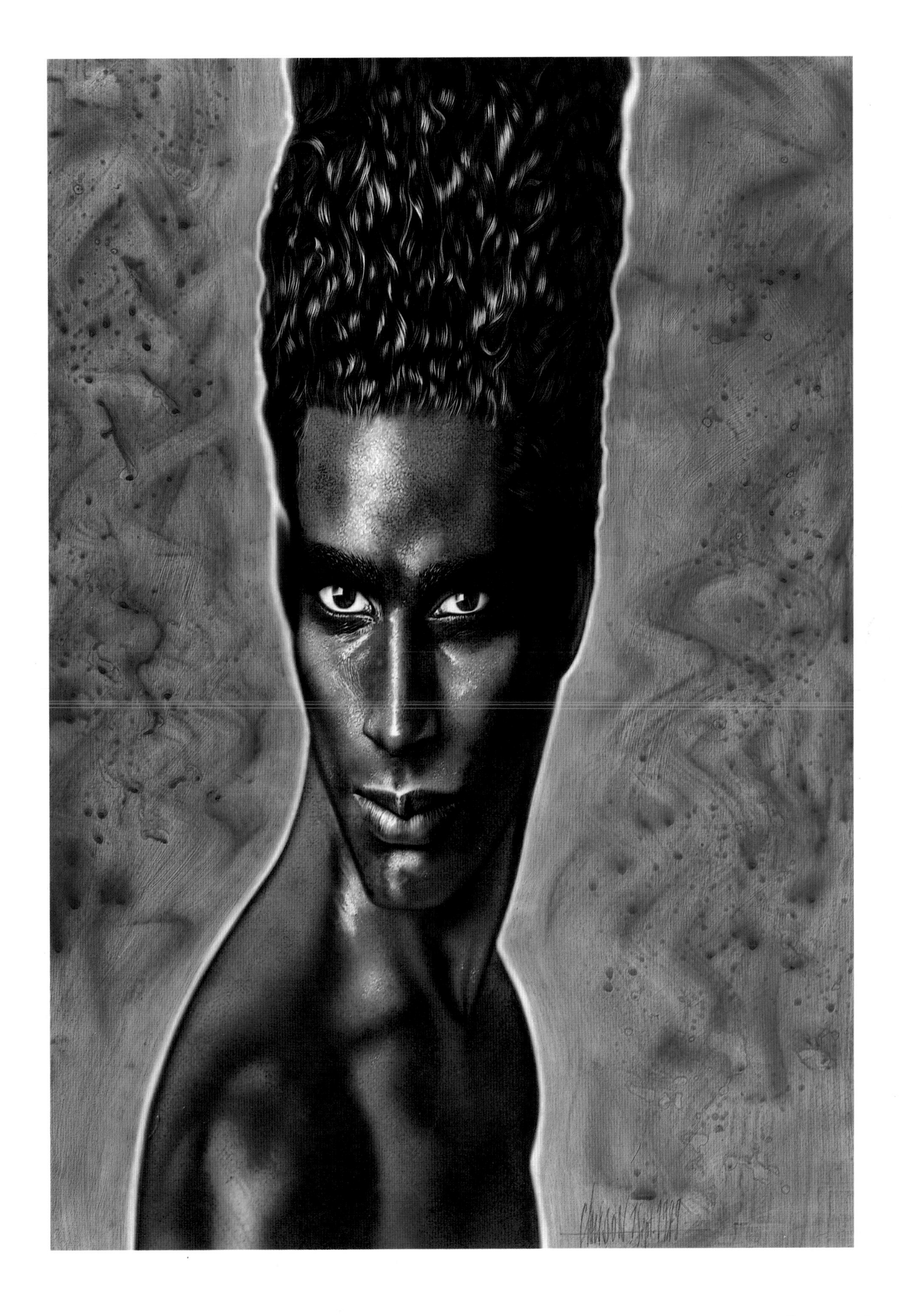

## JULIAN WILLIS

Route de Vaulion 18
CH-1323 Romainmôtier
Tel. 024-53 16 32
Fax: 024-53 16 32

English illustrator established in Switzerland since 1982.
Freelance illustration for advertising, publishing, editorial and television.

Subject: Aerial view of the 18-hole golf course for the Ebel European Masters.
Client: Crans-Montana Golf Club.
Agent: Marc Biver Development – Neuchâtel.

Subject: Wine labels.
Client: Volg Winterthur.
Publisher/Printer: Roth & Sauter SA – Denges/Lausanne.

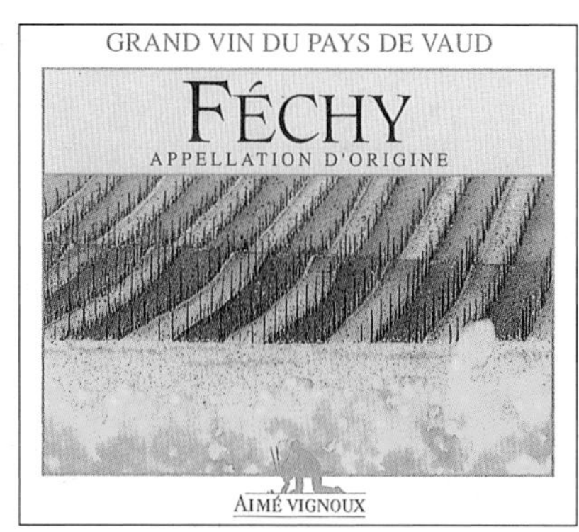


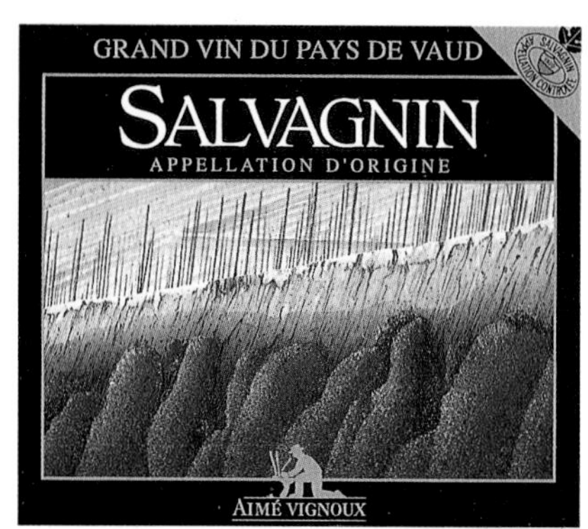

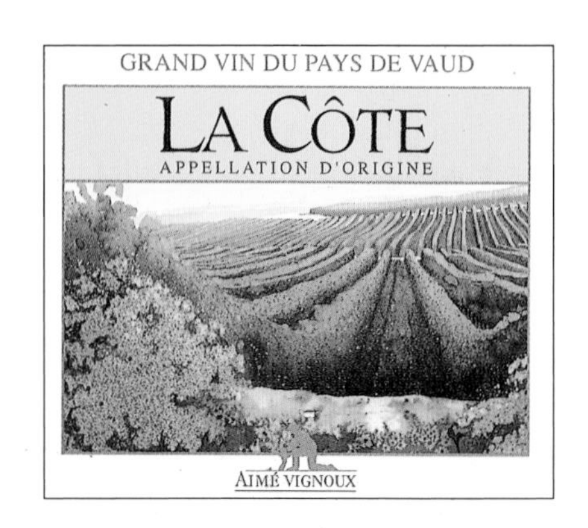

# Illustrators

## Belgium
## Belgique
## Belgien

## MEERSMAN ILLUSTRATORS & DESIGNERS BVBA

Landmolenstraat 13
B-9140 Temse
Tel. 03-771 01 94
Fax: 03-766 20 67

Specialized in: Caricatures, cartoons, portraits, miniatures, airbrush, hyperrealistic illustrations, fashion illustrations, logos...

Specialisaties: Karikaturen, cartoons, portretten, maniaturen, airbrush, hyperrealistische- sfeer- perspektief- modetekeningen, logo's...

Spécialisations: Caricatures; cartoons; portraits; miniatures; aérographe; illustrations de mode, d'ambiance, de produits, -hyperréaliste; perspectives; logos...

Clients / Klanten / Clients:
Euro Shoe Unie, GB/INNO/BM, Roularta, Eternit, Sun Parks, WTCB, Super Club, Ikea, Sicpa, Boelwerf, Gyproc, Interbrew, several Ministries, various ad agencies.

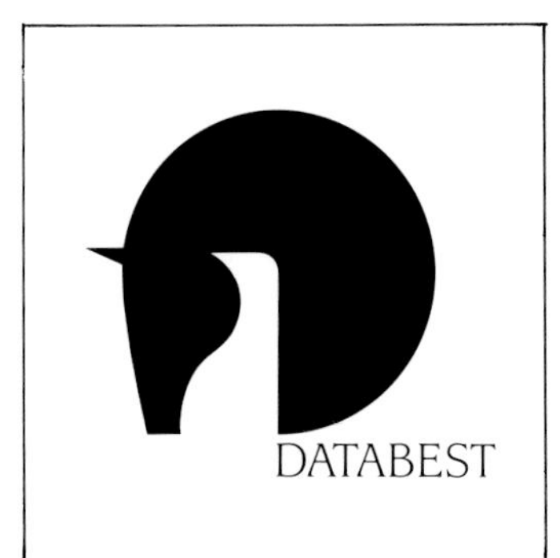

knack
DOSSIER
WATER
De kust - onze rivieren - het slib - het grondwater


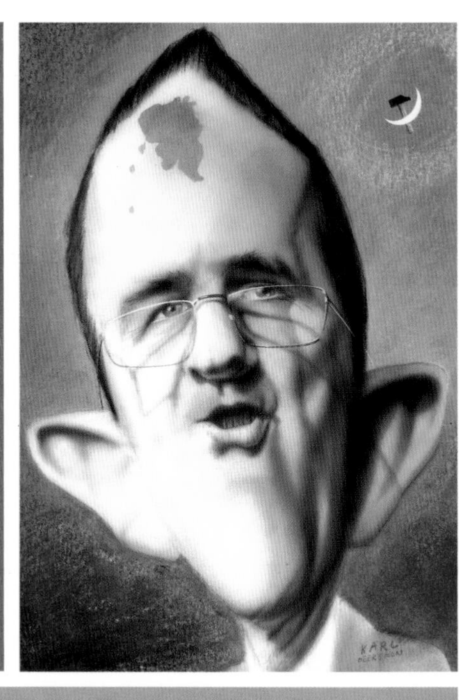

## AEROGRAFICS

MARK VYNCKE
Visserij 72
B-9000 Gent
Tel. 091-23 65 07

Airbrush illustration.
From logo upto photo and TV setting.
Graphic creation.
Photo retouching.

Airbrush illustraties.
Van logo tot en met foto- en TV decor.
Grafisch ontwerp.
Fotoretouche.

Illustrations à l'aérographe.
Du logo aux décors photo et TV.
Création graphique.
Retouche photo.

ENGRAVED BY

COLORSTUDIO
GHENT - BELGIUM

THANKS MARINO BASSO

# FRANKA VAN DER LOO

Binnenkadijk 322
NL-1018 AZ Amsterdam
Tel. 020-23 36 89

1

2

**1** i.s.m. Bob Takes
*Affiche theatervoorstelling*
**2** i.s.m. Karin Mathijsen Gerst
*Illustratie NRC Handelsblad*
**3**
*Coverillustratie 'Mens en Gevoelens'*
**4**
*Illustratie Blad*

3

4

# Illustrators

## Holland
## Hollande
## Holland

# 7 ARTS STUDIOS BV

Wilhelminapark 114
NL-5041 EG Tilburg
Tel. 013-43 27 83
35 53 41
Fax: 013-42 76 45

EXPERTS IN VISUALISING
Top level art-impressions and creative use of images in all kinds of communication.

7 ARTS STUDIOS BV geeft vorm aan uw ideeën. Een team van 9 vakmensen staat hiervoor garant. Experts op het gebied van puur tekenwerk, airbrush, fotografie en decorbouw.

7 ARTS STUDIOS BV is gespecialiseerd in het vervaardigen van art-impressions voor architectuur-presentaties en visuals voor advertising.

## JURGEN WIERSMA

Weth. Frankeweg 26
NL-1098 LA Amsterdam
Tel. 020-92 86 10
Fax: 020-92 86 10

Agents:
THE ARTBOX
Kruislaan 182
NL-1098 SK Amsterdam
Tel. 020-668 15 51
Fax: 020- 93 99 07

STEVEN WELLS
ILLUSTRATION AGENCY
P.O. Box 651
London SE25 5PS
Tel. 081-689 1427
Fax: 081-683 0607

Specialised in meticulous images in oilcolours, on masoniteboard. His illustrations have been used in advertising and editorial work.

Spécialiste d'images méticuleuses à l'huile et sur planche en dur. Ses illustrations sont utilisées dans la publicité et la presse.

Spezialist auf äusserst genaue Ölgemälde, ebenfalls auf Bretterwänden. Seine Illustrationen werden in der Werbung sowie bei der Presse verwendet.

Clients / Kunden: American Express, Nissan, Heinz, Heineken.

# Illustrators

## Italy
## Italie
## Italien

## BORNIA-MONTICELLI

Via Coni Zugna, 7
I-20021 Bollate (Milano)
Tel. 02-661 019 29
351 28 17

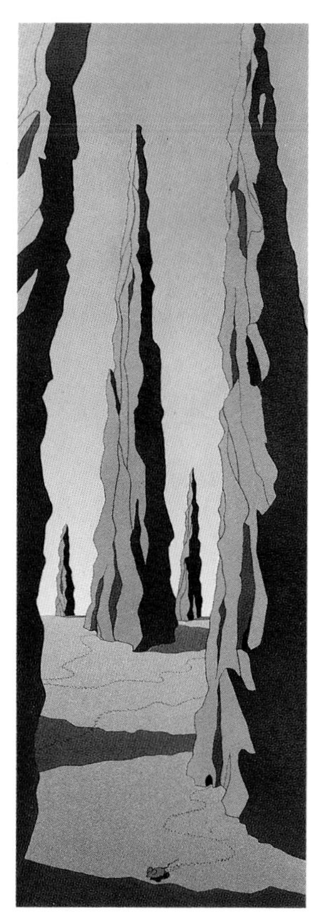

MONTICELLI
BORNIA

# DANA CAMERINI

Corso Italia, 42
I-20122 Milano
Tel. 02-894 022 74
New No. 02-583 113 67

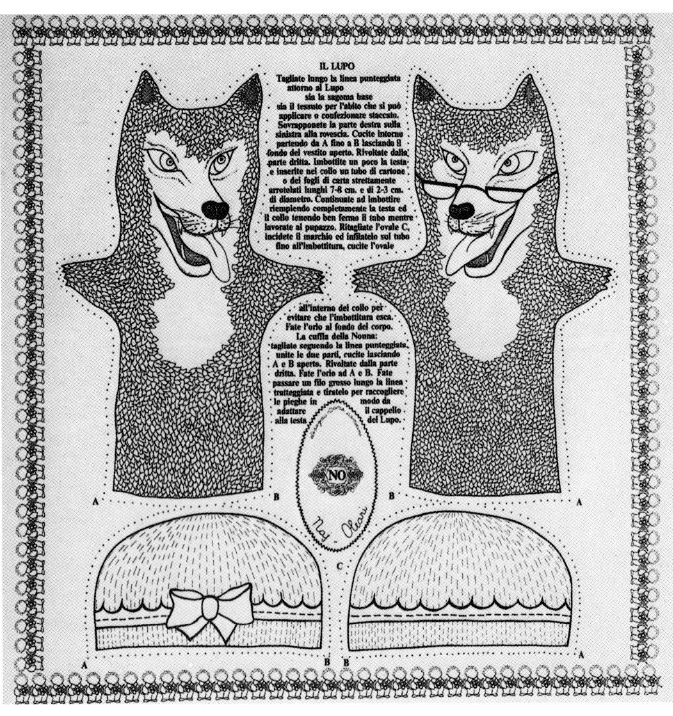

**FIORELLA CAUDURO**

Borgo Tegolaio, 17
I-50125 Firenze
Tel. 055-21 52 04


Title: Anti-fire campaign.

Titolo: Campagna Antincendi.

Titre: Campagne anti-incendie.

## GIAMPIETRO COSTA

Via Calderara, 5
I-37138 Verona
Tel. 045-57 78 33
Fax: 045-57 78 33

Agent:
MILAN ILLUSTRATIONS AGENCY
Via G. Parini, 12
I-20121 Milano
Tel. 02-290 026 32
Fax: 02-657 24 85

Self-promotion.

Auto-publicité.

# PAOLO D'ALTAN

Via Vigevano, 27
I-20144 Milano
Tel. 02-832 18 68

## MICHEL FUZELLIER

Via S. Nicolao, 10
I-20123 Milano
Tel. 02-80 02 94
Fax: 02-80 76 60

Self-promotion.

Promozione personale.

Promotion personnelle.

# PIERLUIGI GATTO

Via Inama, 3
I-20133 Milano
Tel. 02-74 48 37

## RODOLFO GUZZONI

Via Correggio, 14
I-20149 Milano
Tel. 02-49 13 52

1-2. Self-promotion.
3. Pharmaceutical Client Bayer.
4. Self-promotion.

1-2. Promozione personale.
3. Cliente Bayer Farmaceutica.
4. Promozione personale.

1-2. Promotion personnelle.
3. Client Pharmacie Bayer.
4. Promotion personnelle.

1

2

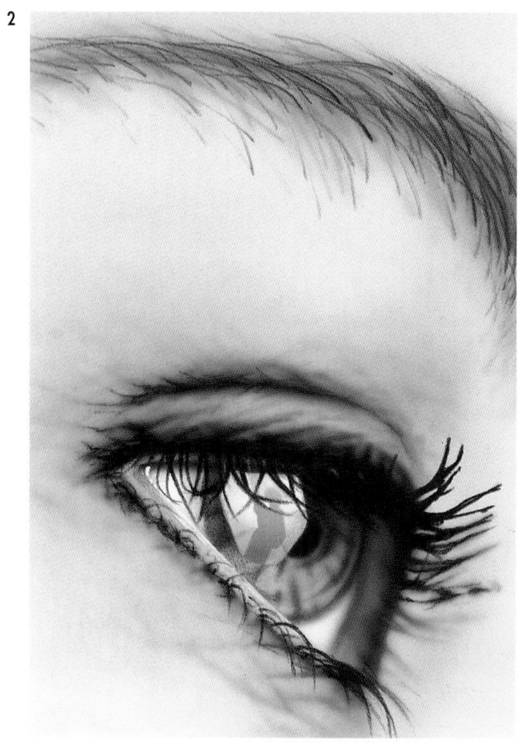

3

4

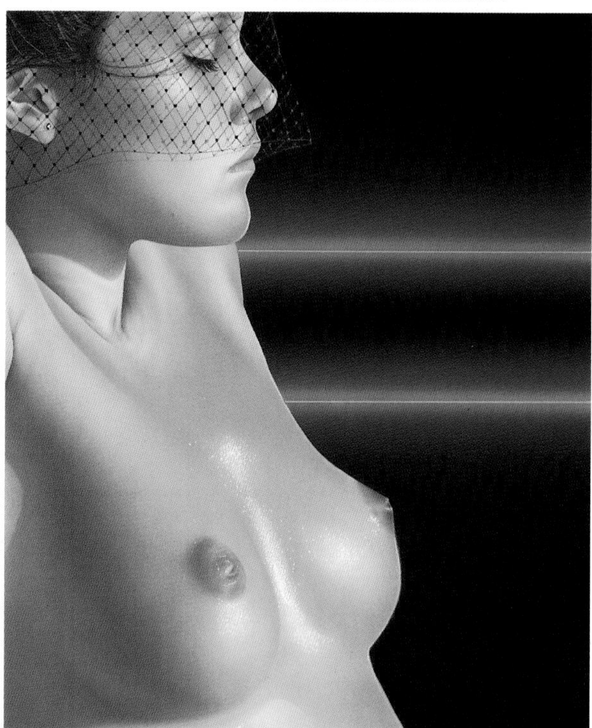

# MARIASTEFANIA RE

Via Correggio, 14
I-20149 Milano
Tel. 02-49 13 52

1-2-3-4. Quaker Chiari e Forti.

1 2 3 4

**STEFANO RIBOLI**

Via Perola, 2/B
I-24021 Albino (Bergamo)
Tel. 035-75 46 07
Fax: 035-75 46 07

New Target Agency.

Agenzia New Target.

Agence New Target.

# MICHELANGELO ROSSINO

Via S. Quintino, 23
I-10121 Torino
Tel. 011-54 90 63

1-2-3. Canard Agency.

1-2-3. Agenzia Canard.

1-2-3. Agence Canard.

1

2

3

# GUIDO ROSA

Via Landoni, 9
I-28100 Novara
Tel. 0321-40 21 46
Fax: 0321-40 21 46

Agent:
ANNA CONTESTABILE
(Solo per Piemonte e Valle d'Aosta)

1-2. Client Ermenegildo Zegna.
3. Editor Rizzoli.

1-2. Cliente Ermenegildo Zegna.
3. Editore Rizzoli.

1-2. Client Ermenegildo Zegna.
3. Editeur Rizzoli.

1

2

3

**FRANCO SODANO**

Via Degli Orti, 9
I-22054 Mandello Del Lario (Como)
Tel. 0341-73 02 91

**ALESSANDRA SCANDELLA**

Via Tantardini, 1/A
I-20136 Milano
Tel. 02-894 060 90

**GIAN CARLO VALLE**

Via Bionaz, 7
I-10142 Torino
Tel. 011-707 22 79

# Illustrators

## Norway
## Norvège
## Norwegen

DEVILLE DESIGN A/S 239

## DÉVILLE DESIGN A/S

Parkveien 62A
N-0254 Oslo 2
Tel. 02-44 24 80
Fax: 02-55 18 20

Since 1988, Déville Design A/S
Graphic Design & Illustration
Stian Bråthen
Ellen Rongstad
Nippe Pahle

Desde 1988, Déville Design A/S
Diseño gráfico y ilustración
Stian Bråthen
Ellen Rongstad
Nippe Pahle

# Illustrators

## Portugal
Portugal
Portugal

**JORGE SILVA**
Est. Benfica, 584 1.° Dt.°
P-1500 Lisboa
Tel. 716 39 49

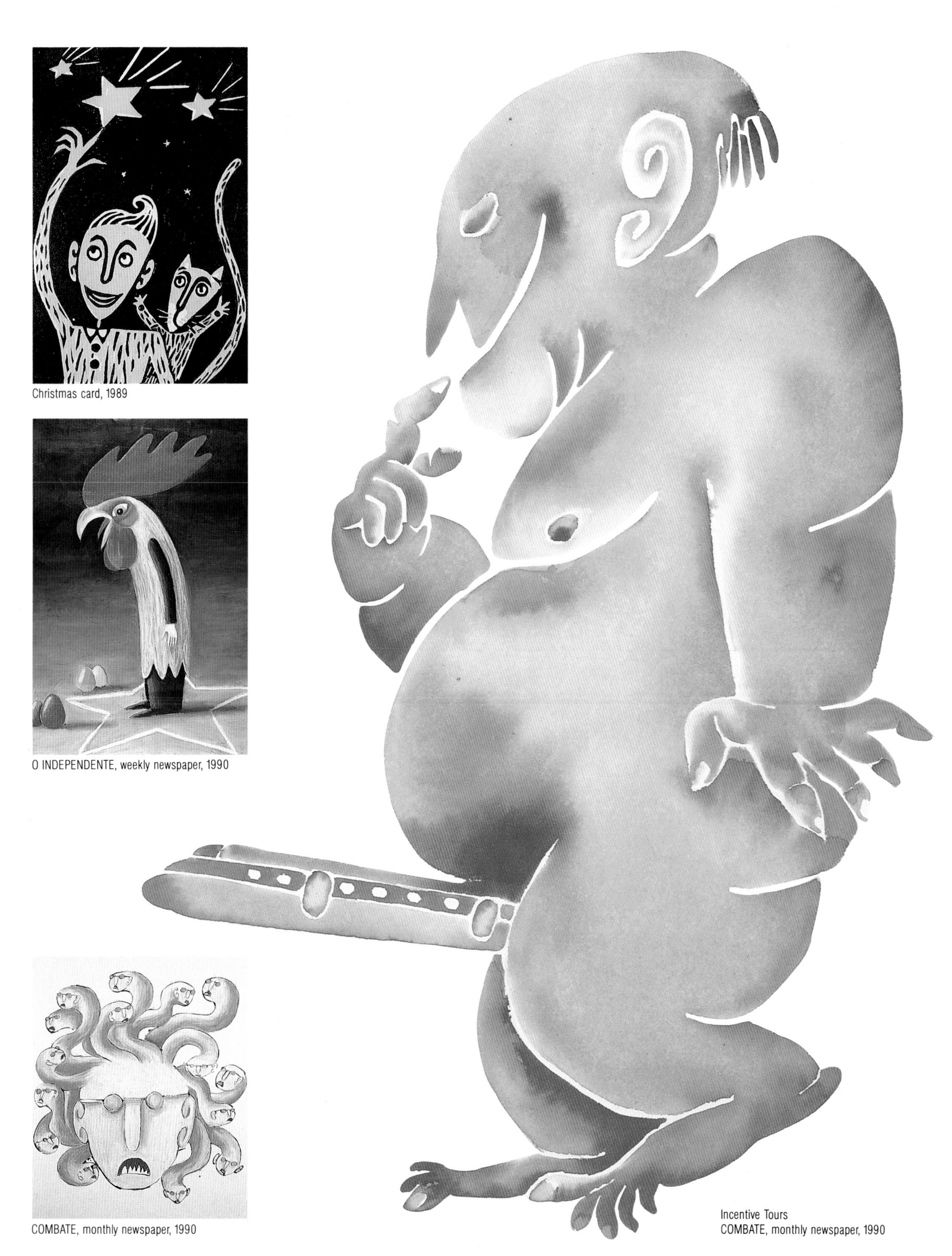

Christmas card, 1989

O INDEPENDENTE, weekly newspaper, 1990

COMBATE, monthly newspaper, 1990

Incentive Tours
COMBATE, monthly newspaper, 1990

# Illustrators

## Spain
## Espagne
## Spanien

## LUIS ALVAREZ

Santa Perpetua, 14 Ent.
E-08012 Barcelona
Tel. 93-218 62 10
Fax: 93-218 62 10

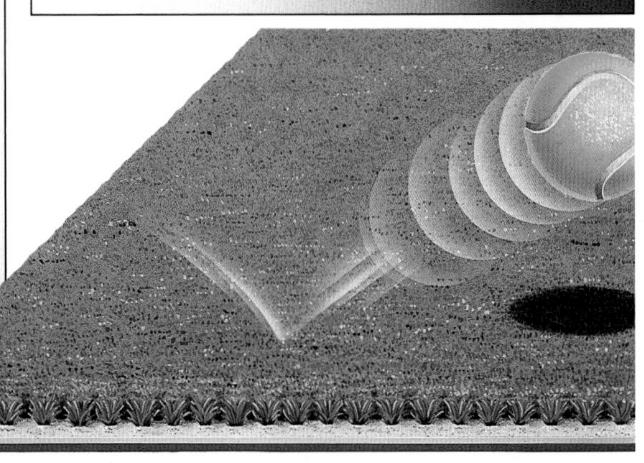

**MIGUEL TRAVIESO**

Plaza de la Cruz, 3
E-47162 Aldeamayor de S. Martin (Valladolid)
Tel. 983-55 69 51

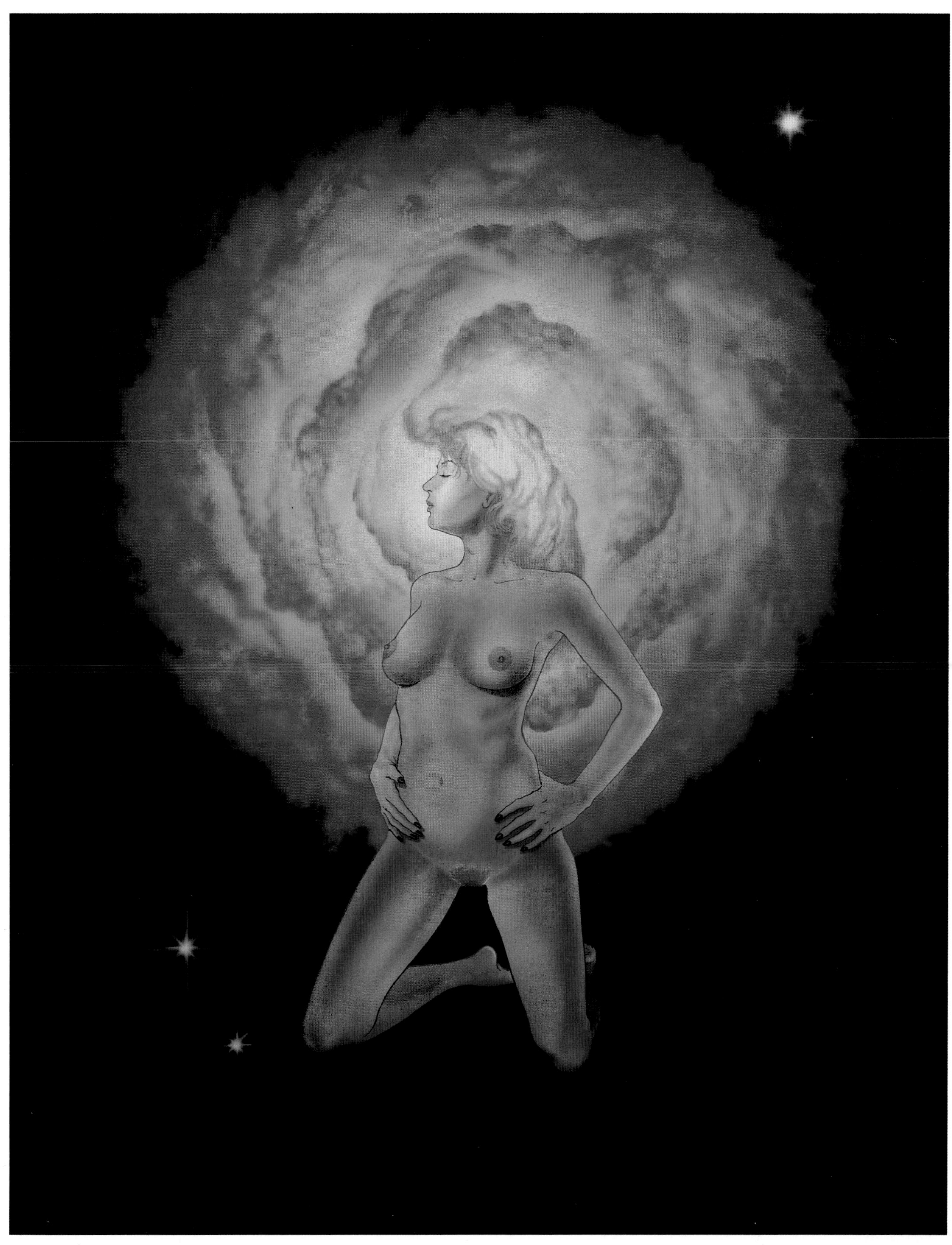

# EUGENIO RAMOS

Plaza Olavide, 5
E-28010 Madrid
Tel. 91-448 24 04
Fax: 91-448 51 46

# ALBERT ROCAROLS

Rosellón, 148-5.º 2.ª
E-08036 Barcelona
Tel. 93-454 29 71

Represented in USA by:
S.I. International – HERB SPIERS
43 East 19th Street
New York, NY 10003
Tel. 212-254 4996
Fax: 212-995 0911

**JOAN RIGAU**

Avda. Coll del Portell, 59 B
E-08024 Barcelona

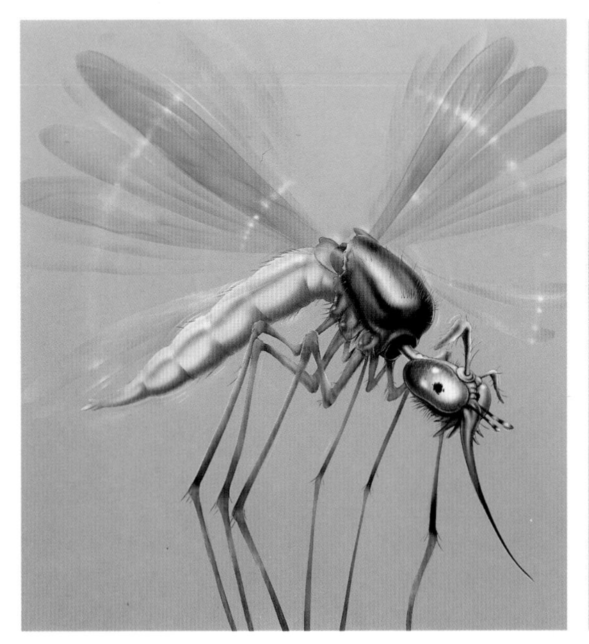

## SANTIAGO LERIA

Gran Vía, 80, 2.°
E-28013 Madrid
Tel. 91-247 22 51
247 76 00 (Ext. 48)
Fax: 91-247 22 51

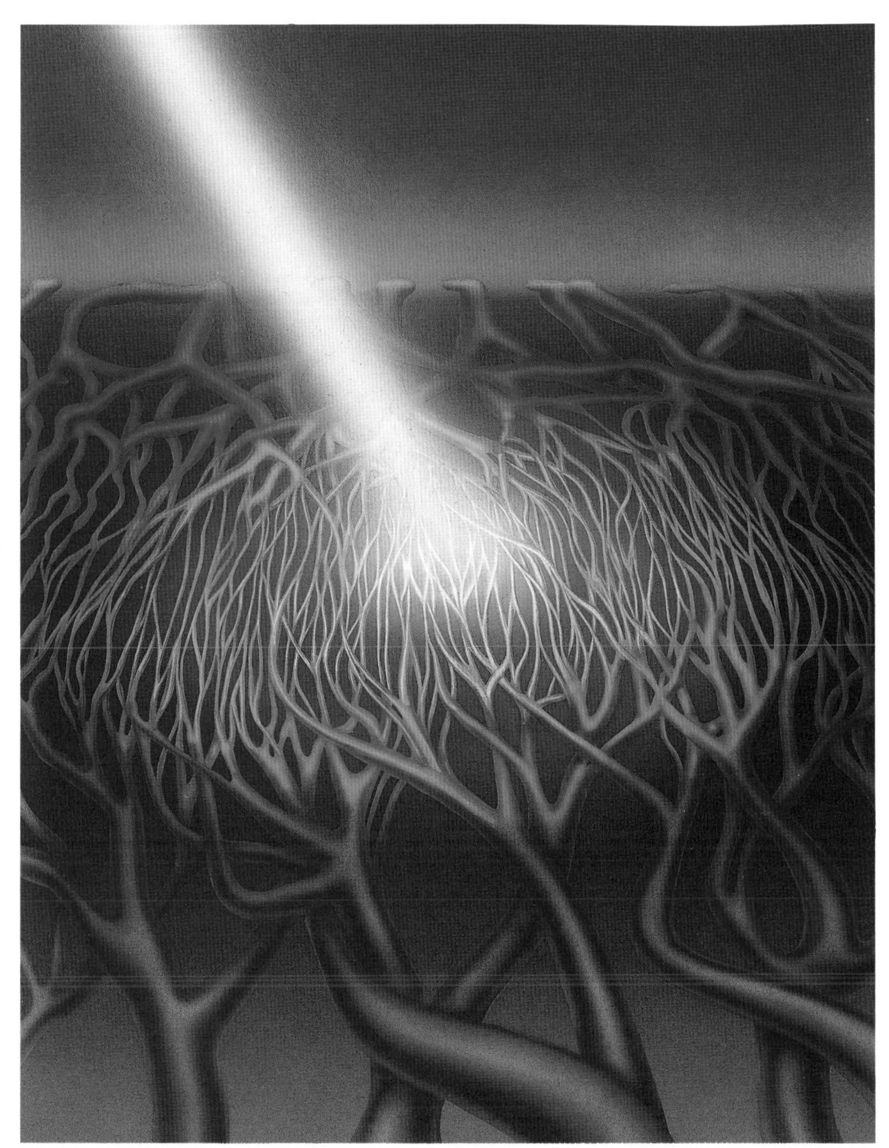

"MICROCIRCULACIÓN PERIFÉRICA"

PROGRAMA DE NAVIDAD

"ZUMO DE MANZANA"

FELICITACIÓN NAVIDEÑA

CARTEL

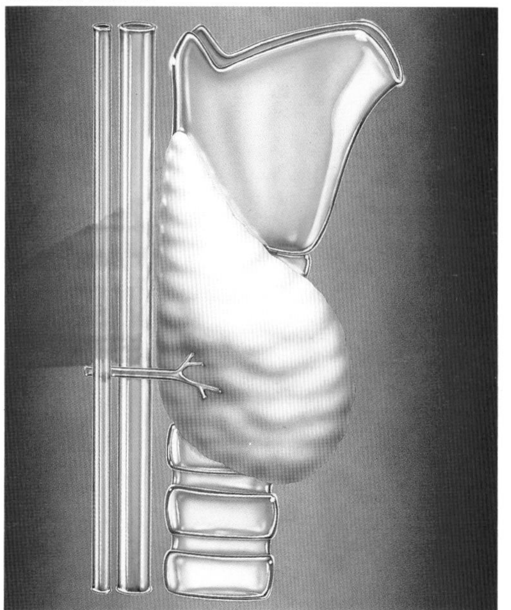

"GLÁNDULA TIROIDES"

# HUMBERTO DIAZ SANTANA

Victor Andrés Belaúnde, 9-2.º Izq.
E-28016 Madrid
Tel. & fax: 430 57 54

Realiza sus estudios en su ciudad natal, Buenos Aires, en las Academias de Bellas Artes Augusto Bolognini y Prilidiano Pueyrredón. Cursa estudios en técnica Publicitaria y Diseño Gráfico.
En España (1978) se especializa en técnica de aerografía. Primeramente en el campo editorial, donde editarán sus trabajos en revistas como Lui, Play-Boy, Penhouse, portadas para Cambio 16 y Mercado.
Sus aportaciones derivan al campo publicitario y colabora en agencias como: Dardo, Cid Publicidad, Lintas Madrid, J.W. Thompson, Young & Rubicam, Tiempo BBDO, Maketa, Contrapunto, Lemonnier & Tremble, Delvico, Ricardo Pérez, Bassat; estudios gráficos como: Estevez-Morales, RPM, J.R.C.E.C.R., Flash para clientes de renombrado prestigio: Johnson's, Renault, La Casera, Philips, Renfe, Cointreau, Banco Hispano Americano, ERT, Banco Urquijo Unión, Coca-Cola, Gillette, Clesa.
Algunas de sus obras están editadas en publicaciones especializadas en España y en el extranjero.

**HUMBERTO DIAZ SANTANA**

Victor Andrés Belaúnde, 9-2.° Izq.
E-28016 Madrid
Tel. & fax: 430 57 54

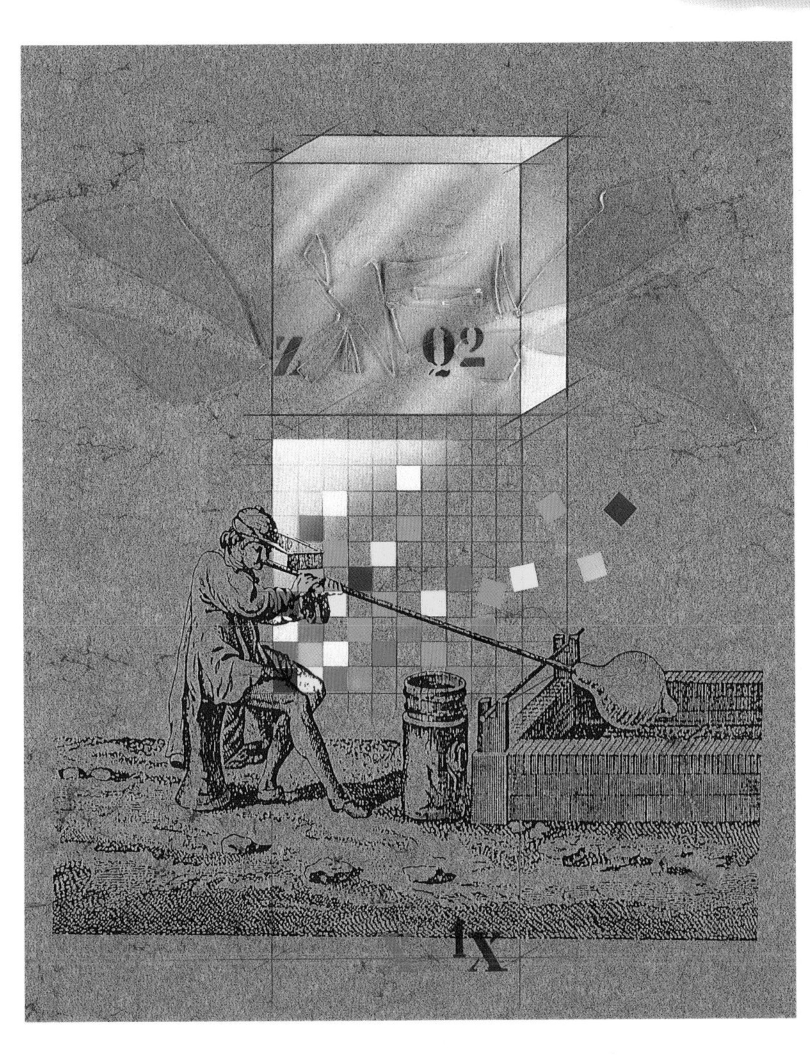


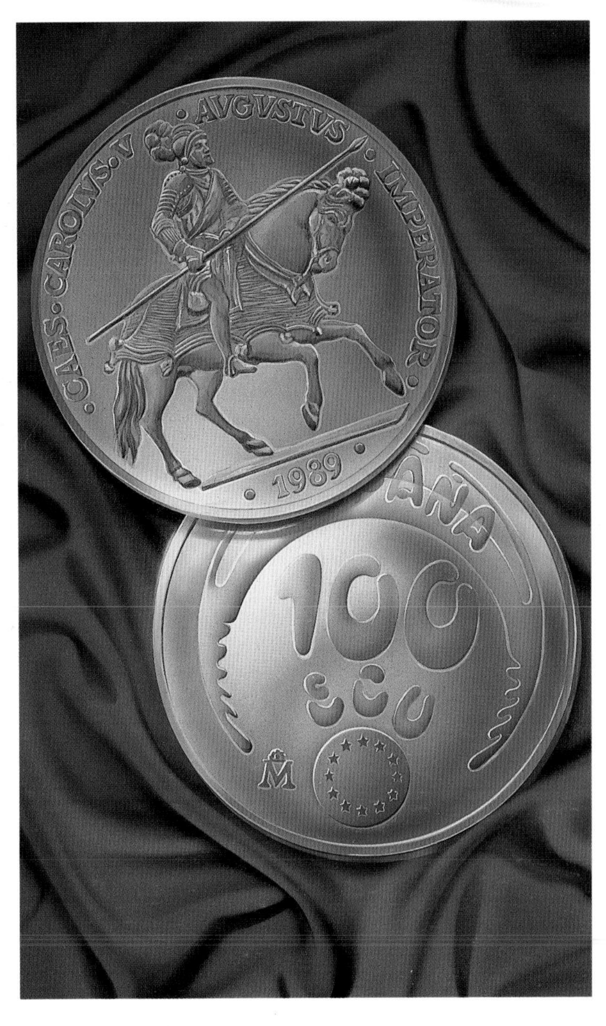

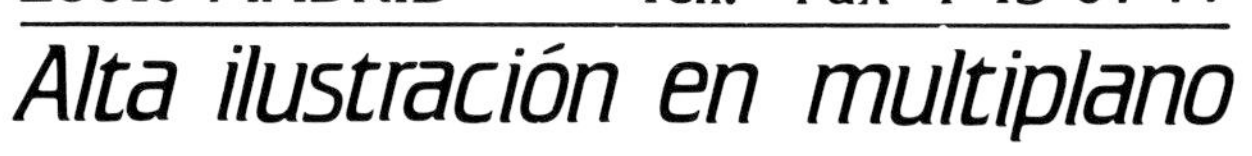


General Alvarez de Castro, 43 - Bajo Dcha.
28010 MADRID Telf. - Fax 4 45 07 77

*Alta ilustración en multiplano*

**JUAN XARRIE**

C/ Gloria, 3
E-28820 Coslada (Madrid)
Tel. 673 76 72
Fax: 673 86 29

RAMON GONZALEZ TEJA ILUSTRADOR

Cartagena 16 · 5°C · Telf. 2451443 · Fax. 2451443 · 28028 Madrid

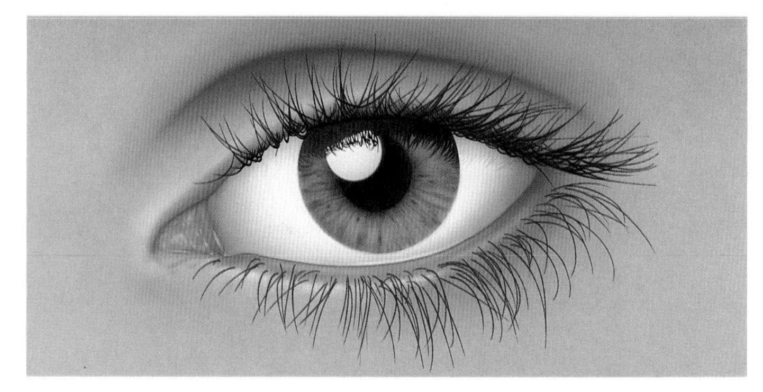

# BEATRIZ DE PEDRO

Cartagena, 131, 5.° 1zda.
E-28002 Madrid
Tel. 564 35 60

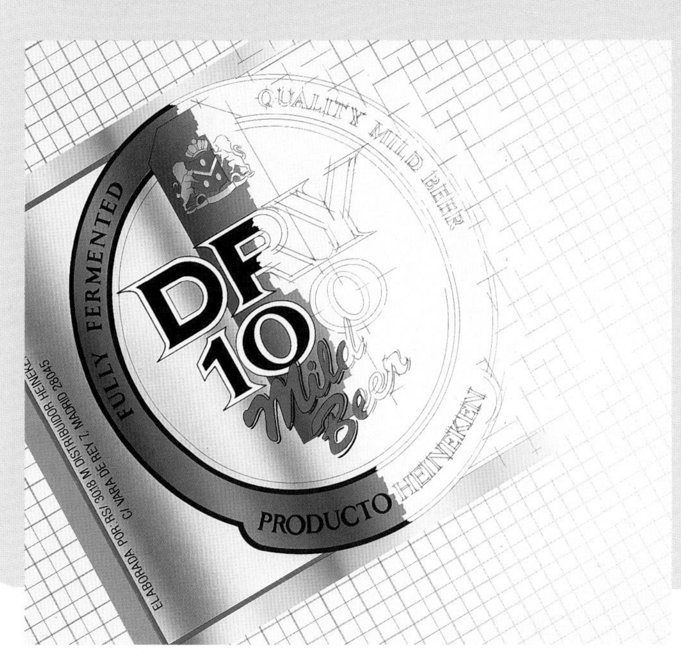

# GAMERO

Acrylic on illustration board: 50 x 70 cm

Acrylic on gesso: 70 x 60 cm

Acrylic on illustration board: 50 x 35 cm

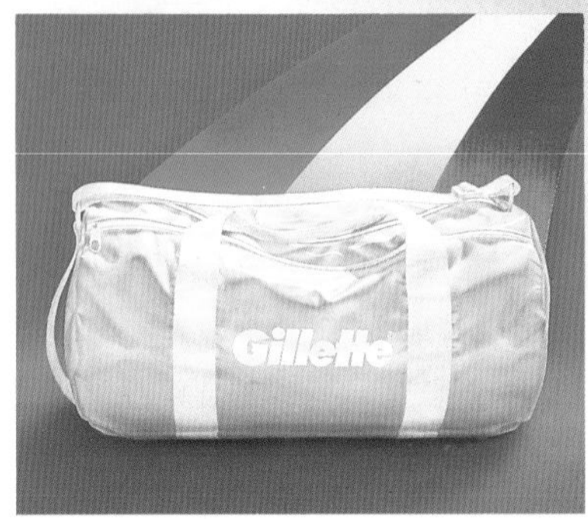


Acrylic on illustration board: 50 x 35 cm

PEDRO
GAMERO
91.437.3313
FAX IN STUDIO
MADRID

FCO. PEREZ FRUTOS (FRAN)

Jaén, 11 Bajo E - 28020 MADRID
Tels. 535 35 84 - 656 08 94

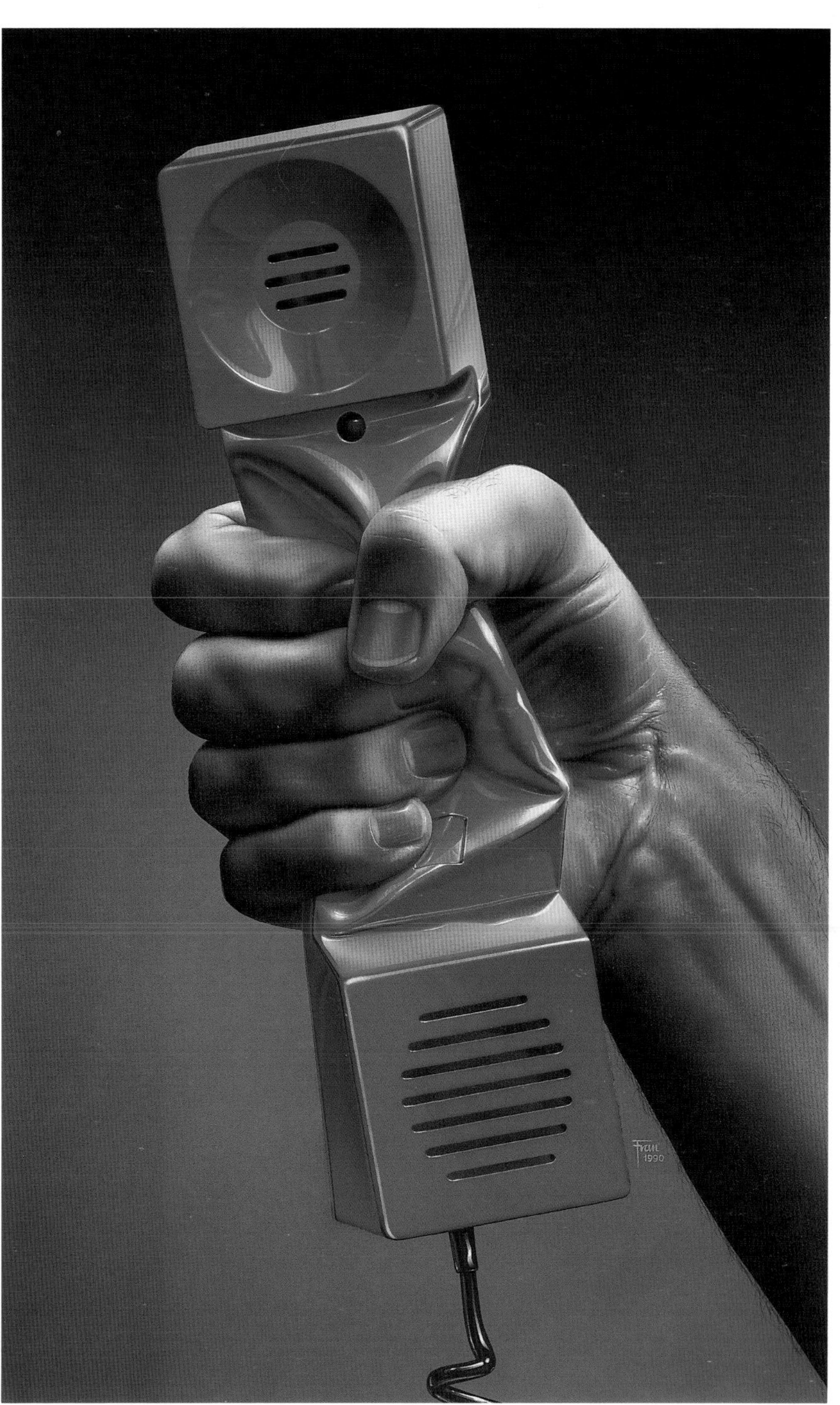

**MIGUEL ANGEL FLORES**
Av. de Francia, 24-3.° C
E-28916 Leganes (Madrid)
Tel. 91-686 45 88

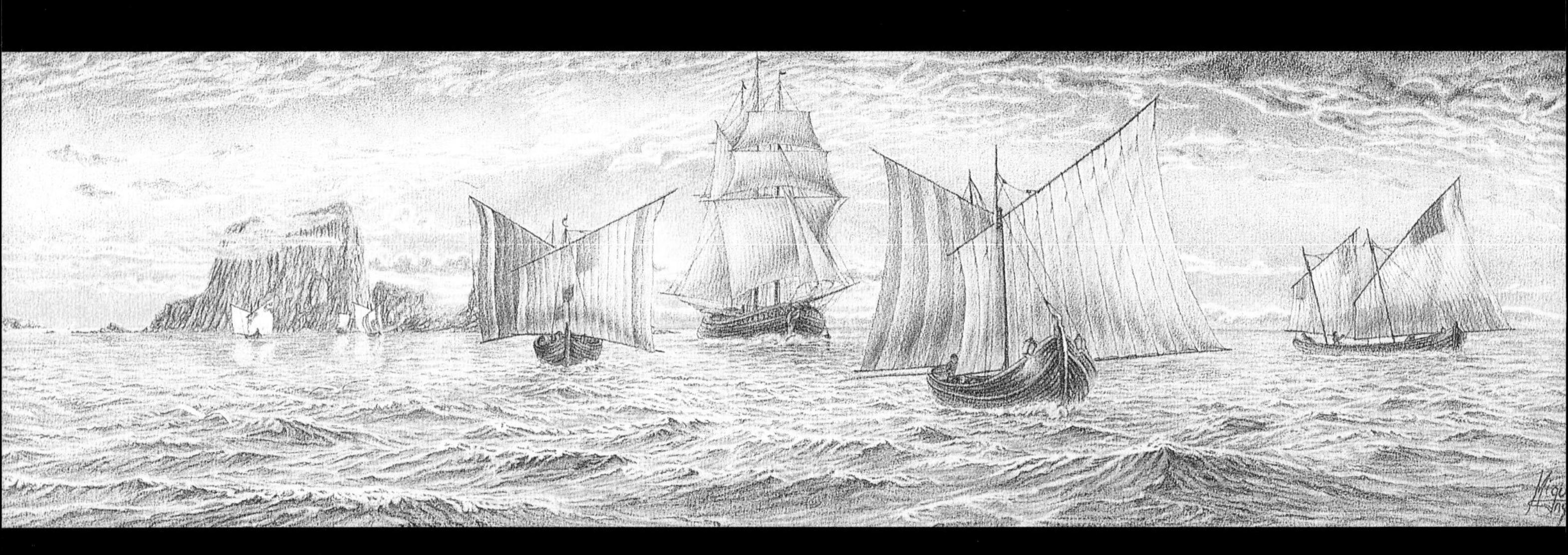

**TEO MOGICA**

Marroquina, 106-7.° B
E-28030 Madrid
Tel. 439 87 95

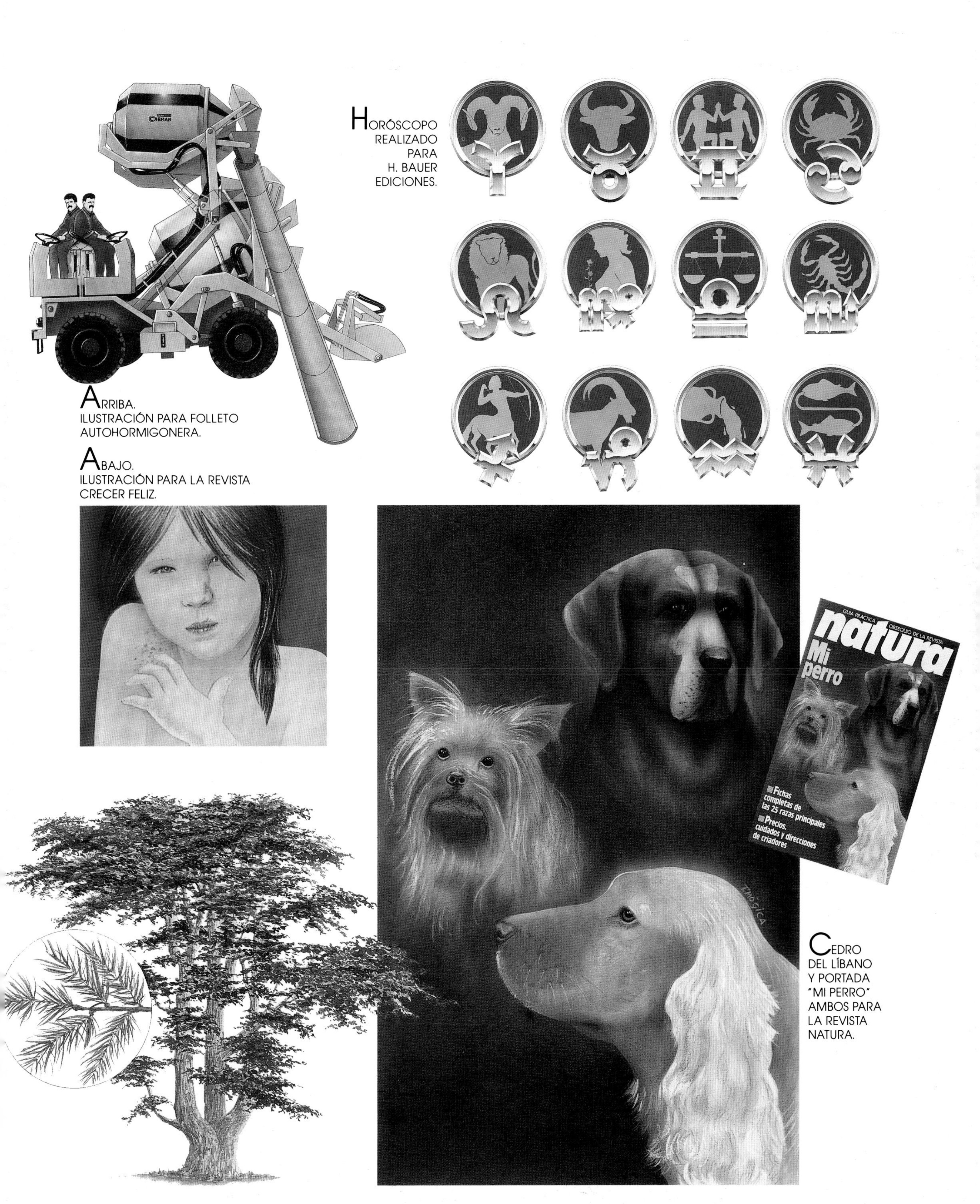


HORÓSCOPO REALIZADO PARA H. BAUER EDICIONES.

ARRIBA.
ILUSTRACIÓN PARA FOLLETO AUTOHORMIGONERA.

ABAJO.
ILUSTRACIÓN PARA LA REVISTA CRECER FELIZ.

CEDRO DEL LÍBANO Y PORTADA "MI PERRO" AMBOS PARA LA REVISTA NATURA.

CALLE DEL PEZ, 12 - 1.° G • 28004 MADRID • TEL. 522 77 34

# ANTONIO IRÚN

Representado en España por
GOLD-2
Dr. Fleming, 26
E-28036 Madrid
Tel. 457 73 97
Fax: 563 49 99

Clientes:
Coca-Cola; Banco Herrero; Banco Atlantico; Peugeot; General Motors; OB; Pepsi-Mirinda; Tudor; MMT-Seguros; Porsche; IBM; Camel; Pall Mall; L'Oréal; Race.

ANTONIO IRUN

# GERARDO AMECHAZURRA

Representado en exclusiva por
GOLD-2
Dr. Fleming, 26
E-28036 Madrid
Tel. 457 73 97
Fax: 563 49 99

Clientes:
Bassat, Ogilvy & Mathers;
D'Arcy, Massius, Benton & Bowles;
G + J Editorial; Z Editorial; JWT;
Publicidad 96; Grupo 16; BSB.

# M. OVILLO

foto retocada

foto original

**RETOQUE DE FOTOGRAFIA**
**AEROGRAFIA**
**Tfno. 7115610**
**4621183**

foto retocada

foto original

ilustración con acrilico sobre carton 50 x 70

ilustración con acrilico sobre carton 70 x 100

# ENRIQUE ROURA

Calle Joaquín Costa, 51
E-28002 Madrid
Tel. 91-563 99 02

# MIGUEL A. GIL / GUSTAVO GIL


Pº Castellana, 266 - 5.º C
Madrid
Tel. 314 76 35

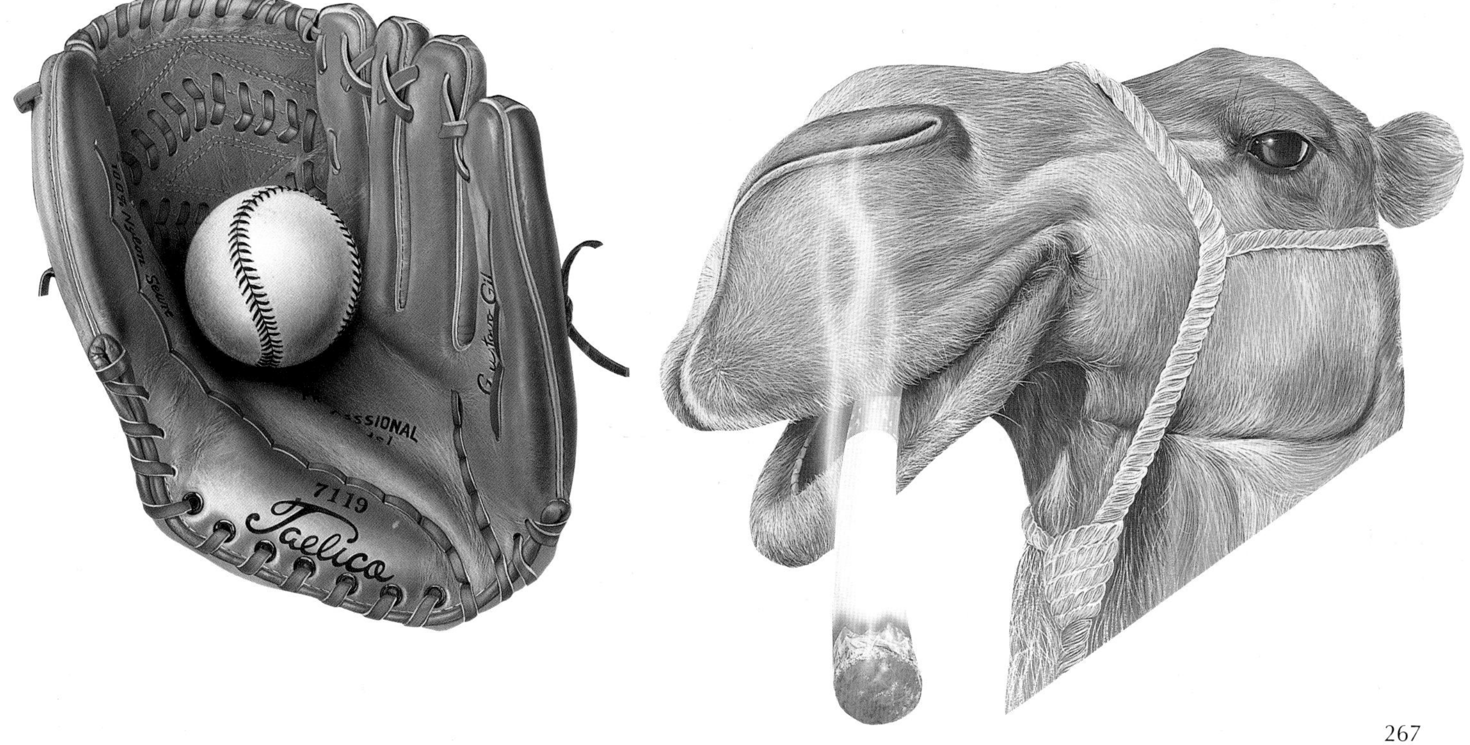

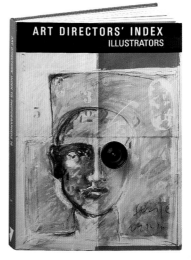

# Illustrators

## United Kingdom
## Grande-Bretagne
## Grossbritannien

## JOHN CHAMBERLAIN

14 Telston Close
Bourne End
Bucks SL8 5TY
Tel. 06285-21941

Clients include:
The Prudential, Legal & General, Chicago First, Blue Star, Hunting, Phillips, Ford, Cummins, Japan Airlines, SAA, Metal Box, British Steel, NEC.

# DUNCAN GUTTERIDGE

15 Wokindon Road
Chadwell-St-Mary
Grays
Essex RM16 4QT
Tel. 03752-3867
Fax: 03752-6169

I specialise in highly finished figurative illustration in airbrush, acrylics, oils or watercolour, working in all areas of the advertising, video and publishing markets.

Je suis spécialisé dans les illustrations figuratives de haute qualité à l'aérographe, acrylique, huiles ou aquarelles, travaillant dans tous les domaines de la publicité, de la vidéo et du marché de l'édition.

Specialisiert in hoch-detaillierten, bildlichen Illustrationen in Airbrush, Acrylic, Öl- oder Wasserfarbe, arbeitet auf allen Gebieten des Werbungs, Video- und Verlagsmarktes.

# STEVE JONES

THE PORTFOLIO GALLERY

22 Bangor Street
Port Dinorwic
Gwynedd LL56 4JD
Tel. 0248-671459

Home address:
33 Brynffynnon Road
Portdinorwig, Gwynedd
North Wales LL56 4SX
Tel. 0248-671209

# RICHARD GRAHAM ECKFORD

Stickleys Barn Minchington
Near Blandford
Dorset DT11 8DH
Tel. 072-551 6320

Hello!

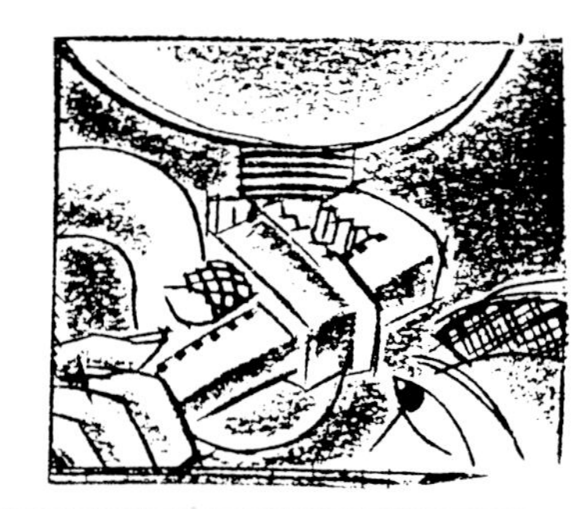

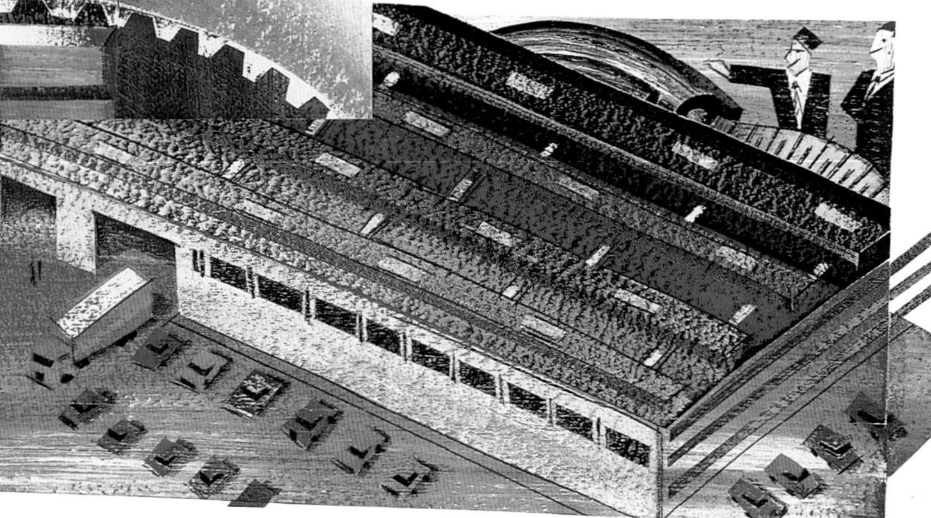

# GRAHAM SMITH

TECHNICAL ILLUSTRATOR

57 Rothschild Road
Chiswick
London W4 5NT
Tel. 081-994 6115

Commercial and industrial, airbrush and line illustrations.

Clients include:
Rank, BMW, Honda, BAT, Sony, British Leyland, Fiat, Canon, Butlins, British Aerospace, Pearce Construction, Instron, General Motors, Dixons, Unilever, GEC, ICI, Telecom...

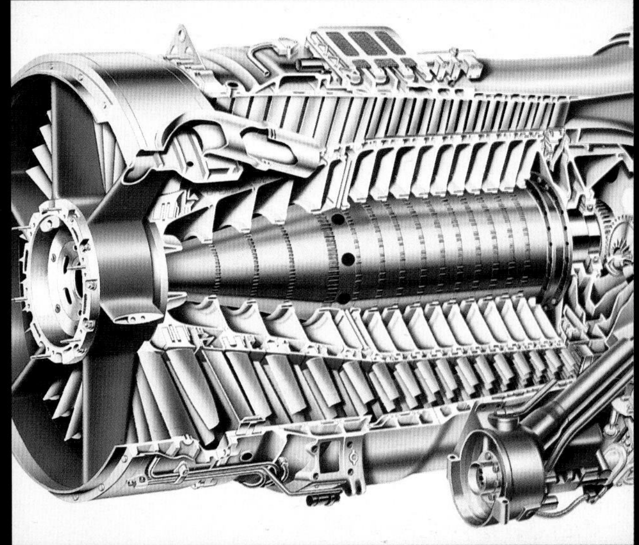

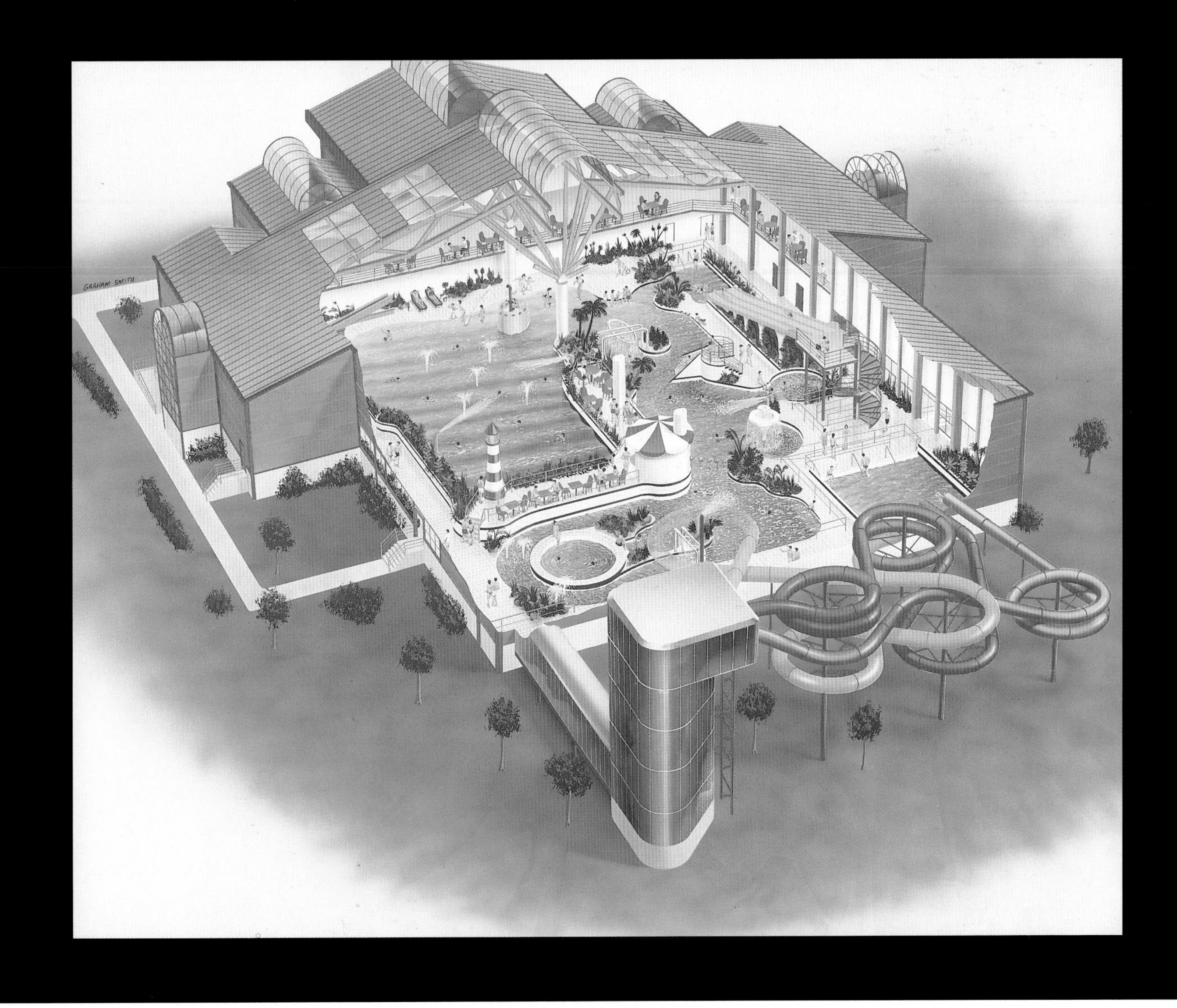

# ARTHUR PHILLIPS

16 Broomfield Road
Surbiton
Surrey KT5 9AZ
Tel. 081-399 5835 (home)
081-547 3299 (studio)
Fax: 081-541 3732

From loose pencil line, various ink-line styles to wash-drawing and airbrush illustration. Subjects usually in a technical direction. Cutaways, ghosted & exploded views my speciality. 17 years experience both home and abroad. I also speak fluent German.

Deutsch sprechender Illustrator mit 17 jähriger Erfahrung im Inland sowie im Ausland. Vom einfachen Bleistiftstrich über verschiedene Tintenstile zu Aquarell und Airbrush-Illustration. Themen im allgemeinen in technischer Richtung. Spezialisiert in Freistellmasken, fantomartigen und explosiven Darstellungen.

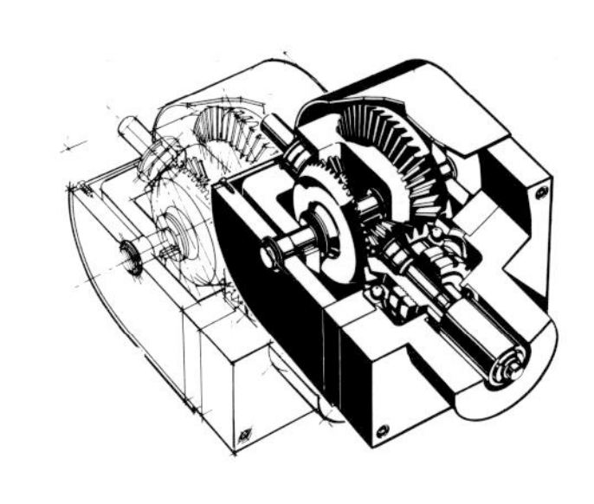

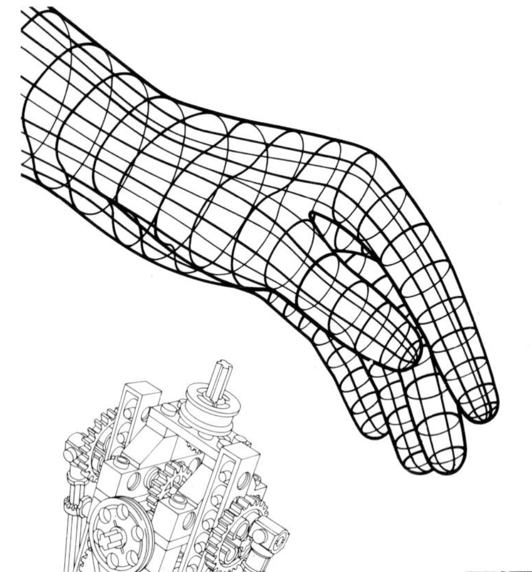

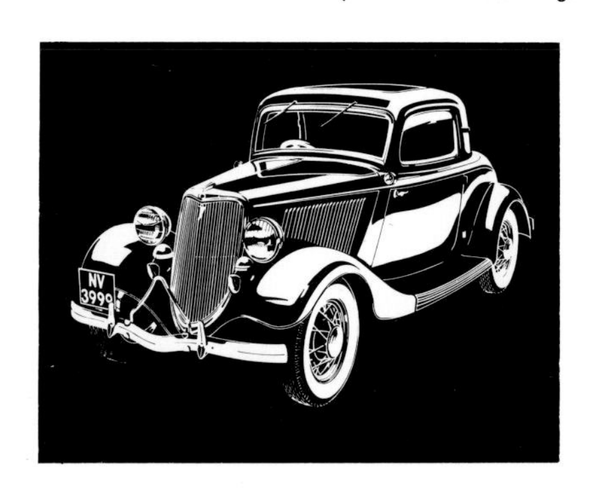


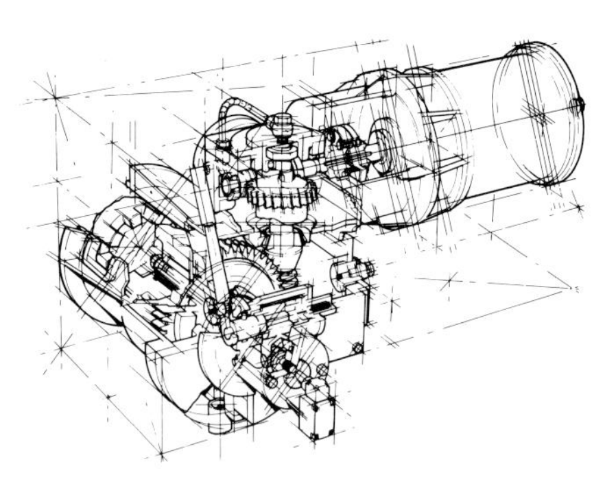

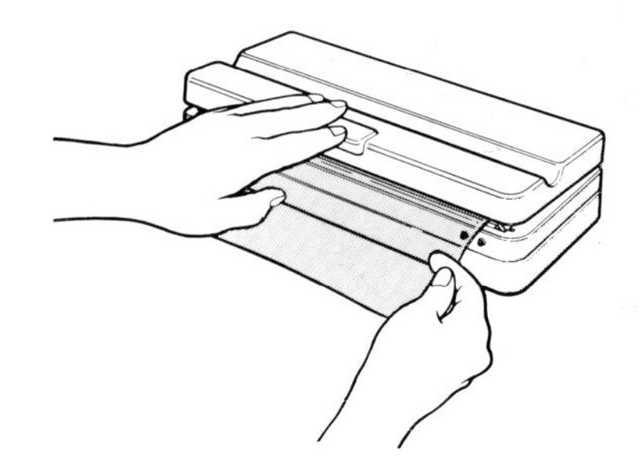

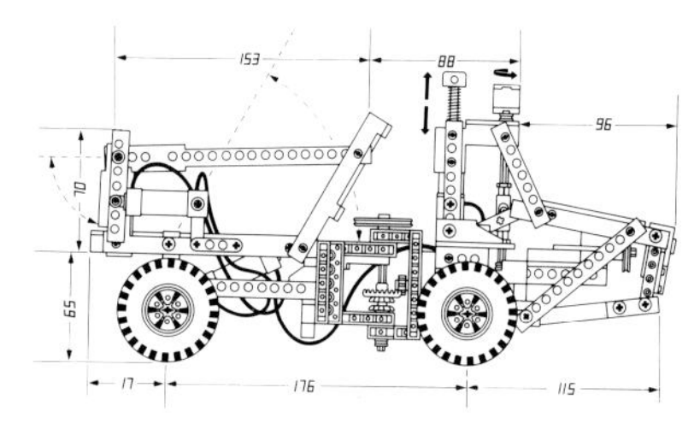

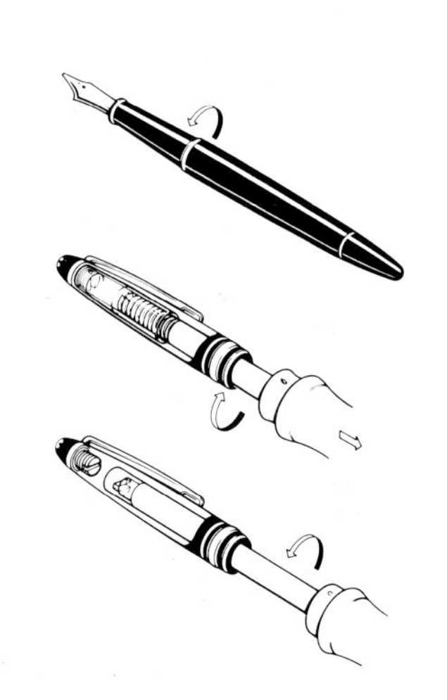

# INDUSTRIAL ART STUDIO

Roger Full
INDUSTRIAL ART STUDIO
Consols, St Ives
Cornwall TR26 2 HW
Tel. 0736-797651
Fax: 0736-794291

INDUSTRIAL ART STUDIO
Hornsteinstrasse 18
D-8000 München 80
Tel. 089-982 82 82
Fax: 089- 98 11 66

Established since 1972.
Specialising in technical line and airbrush illustrations, design and general illustration for industry, advertising, consumer goods and packaging.
Working throughout Europe, Scandinavia and America.

Eingerichtet in 1972.
Spezialisiert in technischen Linien und Airbrush Illustrationen, Design und generelle Illustrationen für Industrie, Werbung, Lundengüter und Verpackungen.
Arbeitet in Europa, Skandinavien und Amerika.

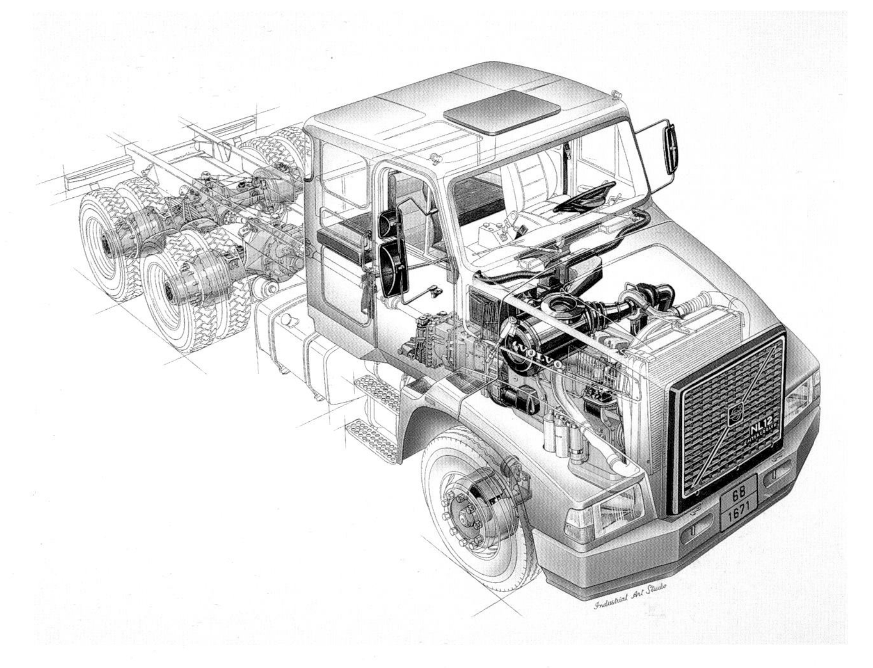


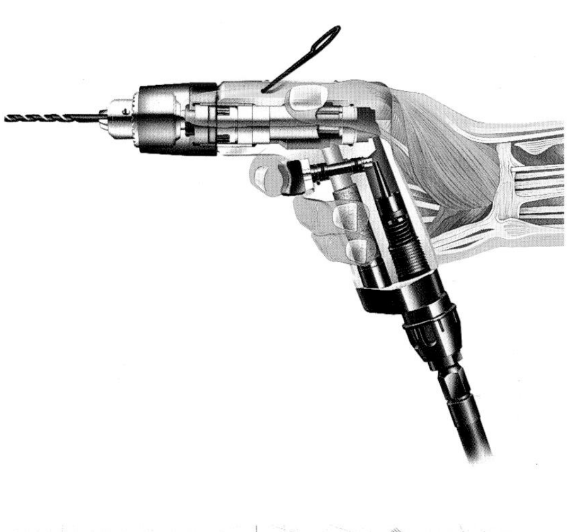

**JOHN LAWRENCE ILLUSTRATOR**

Lower Oakshott Farmhouse
Hawkley, Liss
Hants. GU33 6LP
Tel. 073084220
Fax: 073084246

Outlook Creative Services Ltd., 25 Bruton Place, London W1X 7AB. Tel: 071-499 2610. Fax. 071-355 3761

Design, Direct Marketing, Concepts, Roughs, Storyboards, Animatics, Presentation, Illustration, Lettering, Airbrush, Typography & Mechanical Artwork.

# ARTISTS INC. LTD

7-8 Rathbone Place
London W1P 1DE
Tel. 071-580 66 42
Fax: 071-436 51 83
Agent:
ARTISTS INC. LTD
Tel. 071-580 66 42

We represent a wide range of illustrators with varying styles, but all with one thing in common: quality illustrations to suit your budget. The result? Four years of satisfied customers.

Wir vertreten eine grosse Anzahl von Illustratoren mit verschiedenen Stilen – alle mit der gleichen Aufgabe – Qualitäts-Illustrationen für Ihr Budget. Das Resultat? Vier Jahre zufriedene Kunden.

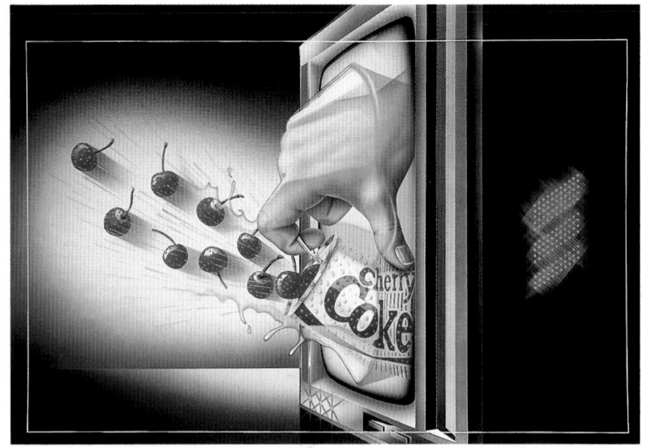


JOHN SPIRES

ET'AL

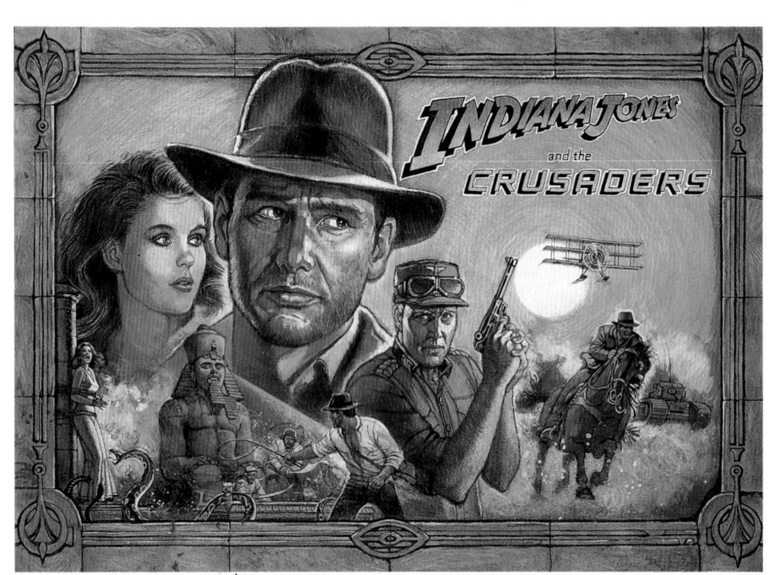


PETER KESTEVEN

PETER HARRIS

TOM DEAREN

IAN SOUTHWOOD

# GARY THOMPSON

Flat 5
47 Ventnor Villas
Hove
East Sussex BN3 3DB
Tel. 0273-204196

Clients include: Art Attack Studios / EMI Records. Creed Lane Studio / The Crown Suppliers. Catchee Monkee Design / Ernst & Young. Redwood Publishing / World Wildlife Fund. And, Oxford University Press.

Sa clientèle comprend: Art Attack Studios / Disques EMI. Creed Lane Studio / Fournisseurs de la Couronne. Catchee Monkee Design / Ernst & Young. Redwood Publishing / WWF. Et, la Presse de l'Université d'Oxford.

Kunden: Art Attack Studios / EMI Schallplatten. Creed Lane Studio / Die Königlichen Lieferanten. Catchee Monkee Design / Ernst & Young. Redwood Publishing / WWF. Und, Universitätspresse von Oxford.

# DAVID TILL

94 Park Avenue South
London N8 8LS
Tel. 081-348 9012

A versatile artist working in varied areas, including advertising, publishing, graphics, press, posters, editorial, educational, etc. Also visualises, designs, illustrates and produces complete projects in the P.R. and promotional fields.

Un artiste versatile travaillant dans divers secteurs, dont la publicité, l'édition, le graphisme, la presse, les posters, l'éducation, etc. Egalement visualise, dessine, illustre et conçoit complètement des projets dans les domaines des relations publiques et de la promotion.

Ein flexibler Knüstler, arbeitet in verschiedenen Gebieten einschliesslich Werbung, Verlag, Graphik, Presse, Posters, Leitartikel, Bildung, etc. Er visualisiert zeichnet, illustriert und produziert auch komplete Projekte im Gebiet der Werbung und Public Relations.

# LESTER MEACHEM

LESTER MEACHEM ILLUSTRATION

73 Mount Pleasant Lane
London E5 9EW
Tel. 081-806 5449

Clients include:
Prudential, Light & Coley, BDFS Group, Paling Ellis KPR, Colin McCadden Design, Mike Shannon & Associates, Haymarket, Collins, Octopus, Emap Maclaren to name but a few.
Please call for a free full colour broadsheet or to arrange to see my book.

# PENNY SOBR

Flat 4
149 Holland Park Avenue
London W11 4UX
Tel. 071-371 6809
Studio address:
Partnership Studio
9 Macklin Street
London WC2B 5NH
Tel. 071-404 8265

Clients include:
Vogue, Rimmel, House of Fraser, Mirabella, Marie-Claire, Abbott Mead Vickers, Young & Rubicam, Sunday Times, Borkitt Weinreich Bryant of New York, Jenkins Group, Vin-Yard Design, Dupoint, Charles of Ritz, Benjamin Dent, Caroline Neville Ass., Octopus Books, New Woman, Cosmopolitan, BBC, Evans May Partnership, European Illustration 90,91.